Clare Richards

© Clare Richards 1987

First Published 1987

Blackie & Son Ltd
Bishopbriggs, Glasgow G64 2NZ
7 Leicester Place, London WC2H 7BP

British Library Cataloguing in Publication Data

Richards, Clare
    According to Mark.
    1. Bible. N.T. Mark——Commentaries
    I. Title
    226'.306   BS2585.3

    ISBN 0-216-92217-8
    ISBN 0-216-92216-X School ed.

Printed in Great Britain by Bell & Bain (Glasgow) Ltd

Preface

I have written this book primarily for those studying the Gospel of Mark for GCSE examinations and partly in response to requests from readers who liked my previous book **According to Luke** but wanted one on Mark. I hope it will interest people engaged in biblical studies at many levels or bible study groups.

Since, according to the National Criteria, the GCSE examination in Religious Studies is 'open to candidates of any religious persuasion or none', it is important that textbooks should avoid indoctrination. I hope I have succeeded in presenting the Gospel in an impartial and objective way. My aim has been to express as clearly as possible both the traditional interpretation of the Gospel of Mark and the results of modern New Testament scholarship. If denominational schools want to supplement the material I have pointed them in the right direction.

The book falls into three parts.

PART A Background This is a simplified historical and geographical background to New Testament times. It places the writing of this Gospel into its context and is useful for reference.

PART B This is **Mark's Story**—a thematic study of his Gospel. Since the Gospel is not a simple biography of Jesus, but a highly sophisticated theological document, it is obvious that we are dealing with difficult ideas. I include, therefore, some demanding material, but over-simplification would only distort the truth. However, I hope that I have been able to present it in simple language and in an attractive way, lightened by illustrations and good spacing. Each theme is divided into four sections for clarity.
1   *The Way In* which introduces the theme.
2   *Main Issues* which contains the basic facts on the topic.
3   *Looking Deeper* which examines the texts more closely and takes a look at the difficult questions raised by the text.
4   *Questions and Things to Do* which take into account the requirements of the Examining Boards for *Course Work*. The questions are grouped to offer examples covering the three assessment objectives. (Knowledge, Understanding, Evaluation.)
Part B concludes with a page of Questions (page 94) based on specimen exam papers.
I recommend using the *Good News Bible* alongside this book. All biblical quotations are taken from it. It is always useful if students can have their own copy, to be marked as they wish. It is essential that they get to know the actual text of Mark.

PART C Mark for Today. Since Christians believe that the Gospel still speaks to the world today, students will need to examine this section. It is in any case related to those papers in the syllabuses which study contemporary issues. It is in no way a comprehensive study, but may provide useful material for discussion and course work. All the questions in this section are of the 'evaluation' type.

Acknowledgments

The author would like to thank Sr Mary Cluderay of Notre Dame High School, Norwich for her encouragement and help in the preparation of this book.
The author and publishers are grateful to the following for permission to reproduce copyright material.

Text

All the quotations from the Old and New Testaments are from the *Good News Bible*, © American Bible Society 1966, 1971, 1976 published by the Bible Societies and Collins.
Stainer and Bell Ltd for *Who do men say that I am?* by Cecily Taylor © 1974, page 90
We regret that we have been unable to trace the copyright holder of *We plough the fields and scatter* by Jeremy Taylor, page 119.

Photographs

John Fisher cover, pages 2, 10, 24 top, 28, 42, 44, 50, 68 top, 79 top, 99, 100, 107, 108, 110 top
Barbara Norris pages 1, 9 bottom, 68 bottom, 72, 109 bottom left
BIPAC pages 7, 9 top left, 13 bottom left, 13 bottom right (photographer, Richard Nowitz), 16 (photographer Adam Greene), 23 top, 33, 66 bottom, 113 (photographer Z Radovan)
Syndication International pages 8 bottom left, 19 left, 22, 29, 35, 39, 47 top, 55 top, 95, 104 lower left, 106 left, 114 bottom left
UNRWA pages 8 bottom right, 12, 24 bottom (photographer George Nehmeh), 31 (photographer Kay Brennan), 34, 36 (photographer Kay Brennan), 40, 41 (photographer George Nehmeh), 58 top (photographer Munir Nasr), 58 bottom, 66 top (photographer Odd Urbohm), 76 left (photographer George Nehmeh), 76 right (photographer Munir Nasr), 79 bottom, 98 (photographer Munir Nasr), 116, 118
Alan Johnson page 9 top right
Sylvia Turner page 13 top
Victoria and Albert Museum page 17 (by courtesy of the Board of Trustees)
Pierrsha Kurancie of Canon Palmer RC High School page 19 right

The Mansell Collection Ltd pages 21, 53, 73 left
Eastern Daily Press pages 30, 32, 55 second top, 69, 109 bottom right, 111, 114 top, 115
CAFOD page 38 (photographer Sean Sprague)
Aberdeen Press and Journal page 43
David and Jill Wright page 47 bottom
Gerry Mulligan page 49
The Trustees, The National Gallery page 52
Simon McBride/Radio Times page 55 bottom
Carlos Reyes, Andes Press Agency page 56
The Hunterian Museum, Glasgow page 60
Bob Thomas Sports Photography page 62
GENT, Museum voor Schone Kunsten page 71
Anna Dimascio page 80
Simon Talbot page 84
Taizé Community page 86
Accademia Carrara, Bergamo page 90
Stewart Ferguson page 101
Glasgow Herald page 104 top
The Guardian page 104 bottom right (supplied by Christian CND)
Tear Fund page 106 right
Martin Clark page 110 bottom
Mary Anne Felton page 114 bottom right
CR Doughty page 119

Any photograph not acknowledged above was supplied by the author.

Illustrations

Julie Hogan pages 6, 22, 26, 65 (nos 2–4), 81, 112, 117
Doreen Wadham pages 31, 77
Nick Raven page 59

All maps and remaining illustrations by the author.

Contents

Part A

Background

A1 About Jesus

Somewhere in your town you will almost certainly have seen cars bearing the sticker *Thank God for Jesus*. Or you may have seen a poster on the wall, as in the picture. Who was this Jesus? How did he save sinners? How is he supposed still to be saving them? Why thank God for him?

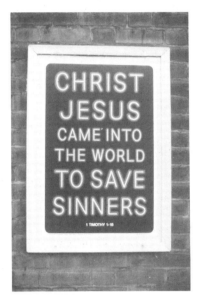

There is probably no one in the history of mankind who has had as much written about him as this man, Jesus. This is one more book.

Who was he? Jesus was a Jew of the 1st century whose life was most ordinary. He was born to a peasant woman, Mary, in Palestine. His life as a carpenter was lived out in a remote village called Nazareth. For three years he went from place to place preaching a message that made him increasingly unpopular. Eventually even his friends left him. He died a dramatic, miserable death. After a false trial, he was given the death sentence and hanged along with other criminals.

Hundreds of people meet tragic deaths, every day. They are soon forgotten. So why was Jesus remembered? Why is his name on car-stickers nearly 2000 years later? What was he preaching about that made him so unpopular?

Jesus was a Jew. The Jews had a firm belief that they had been chosen by God to play a special role in the history of the world. However in Jesus' time it was not clear what this role ought to be. His country was occupied by the Roman army. What could it mean to be God's Chosen People in such circumstances?

Jesus had a clear answer and preached it fearlessly. His vision of God and God's relationship to mankind led to his own death, but it also changed the course of history.

A2 The New Testament and the Gospels

Those who accepted this new vision of God and the demands it made upon themselves, could not help but see that the ordinary man who preached it was really quite extraordinary. They called him 'The Christ' (God's Chosen One). So they were nicknamed 'Christians'.

Early writings about Jesus

Not very much was written down about Jesus at first. Most people couldn't read, so the best way to let people know about him was to *tell* them.

This was done by the preaching of Jesus' earliest followers. Most prominent among these was *Paul*, who carried the message of Jesus through the whole Mediterranean world. The letters he wrote between AD 50 and AD 60 to the Christian communities he had set up are the earliest records we have of Jesus. They now form nearly one-third of what was later called the *New Testament*. Other early disciples added their own writings, sometimes called *Epistles*.

At the same time stories about Jesus and collections of his sayings were being written down, mainly to instruct new followers who had never known Jesus personally. These formed the basis of the four books which we call the *Gospels* of Matthew, Mark, Luke and John. These Gospels make up over one-half of the New Testament.

What is a Gospel?

'Gospel' is an Anglo-Saxon translation of the Greek word 'Evangel'. Both words mean 'good news'. The four Evangelists wrote to express their belief that Jesus was *THE* good news of all time. In Jesus' life and teaching and death, God had revealed himself as never before, and shown himself to be closer to people than anyone could imagine.

The Gospels are therefore not simple biographies, telling readers what happened years ago. They are professions of faith: 'This is what Jesus means to me.' This faith colours every page of the Gospels. The stories they tell (some of them based on history, others on poetry) have all been written to illustrate the faith of the first Christians.

A3 Synoptic Gospels and their writers

Mark, symbolized by the winged lion

The first three Gospels (Mark, Matthew and Luke) are often looked at together. They are called 'synoptic' which means 'look-alike'. If all three are put alongside each other, it can easily be seen how similar they are, both in order and content. In some parts they are absolutely identical. It is quite obvious that they were based on the same collections of sayings and stories about Jesus, although they were written in different places and for different readers.

Mark's Gospel, written about AD 65.

This is the earliest of the Gospels. Although the language is clumsy it is very vivid. Mark was a friend of Peter—one of Jesus' first followers—and it could be that some of Mark's stories come from him. Mark wrote for the Christians in Rome who were undergoing persecution and even death for their faith. His theme is the mystery of Jesus. Who is this man? What does it mean to be 'Son of God'? Mark makes his readers ask these questions over and over again, and insists that they do not give an answer till they see Jesus dying on the cross. In short, he is asking his readers if they are willing to accept martyrdom too.

Matthew, symbolized by the divine man

Matthew's Gospel, written about AD 75.

Matthew took over almost the whole of Mark's Gospel and rewrote it in a different order. At the same time he added a great deal of Jesus' teaching not to be found in Mark, and wove it into the story, as well as other original material. Matthew was writing for the Palestine Jews who had by now become Christians. He presents Jesus to them as the fulfilment of all that the Jewish sacred writings (the 'Old Testament') had looked forward to, almost as a new Moses. Matthew's Gospel is the most repeatable since the Jewish style he used is poetic and repetitious.

Luke's Gospel, written about AD 85.

Like Matthew, Luke copied many of his stories from Mark. He then added the teachings of Jesus which Matthew had used, plus a great deal of new material, making it the longest and most orderly of the Gospels. Luke's Gospel is Volume 1 of a two-part work. His Volume 2 is now called 'The Acts of the Apostles'. This tells how Luke was a friend of Paul, the missionary. Luke was an educated Greek doctor—which means he was a Gentile (non-Jew). He saw the message of Jesus as a joyful proclamation of comforting news for people to hear. Luke's Jesus is a very human, compassionate figure.

Luke, symbolized by the winged ox

> The **Gospel of John** does not fit into the synoptic shape. Though it is based, like the other Gospels, on genuine memories of Jesus, it presents him in a deliberately different light. This is what Jesus has come to mean for someone who has known him a long time. The author, writing probably much later than the others (AD 95?) has chosen his own stories about Jesus. For him, Cana, Lazarus and the rest, all symbolize Jesus' death and resurrection. Many people warm to this Gospel.

John, symbolized by the eagle

A4 More about Mark

In this book we are going to discover what we can about Jesus through the eyes of *Mark*. Now who was he?

It was the tradition of the early Church that he was the companion of Peter, one of the closest friends of Jesus. The most important witness for this is Papias (about AD 100), a disciple of someone called the 'Elder'. Papias wrote:

> *The Elder used to say that Mark, who had been the interpreter of Peter, wrote down accurately all that Peter remembered of what the Lord (Jesus) said and did, though not in order.*

The Mark to whom Papias refers is presumably the Mark mentioned in the letters of Paul and Peter, and perhaps also the John Mark who appears in the Acts of the Apostles. From this early evidence the following picture of our Gospel writer emerges (though not all scholars take Papias' statement to be reliable):

John Mark was the son of Mary, to whose house Peter went when he was delivered from Prison (Acts 12:12–17).

Perhaps Peter had baptized the family, because he called Mark his 'son'. (1 Peter 5:13).

Mark accompanied Paul and Barnabas on their first missionary journey (Acts 12:25; 13:5, 13).

An argument separated Mark from Paul for a time and Mark went to Cyprus (Acts 15:37–39), but he later joined up again with Paul (Philemon 24; Colossians 4:10; 2 Timothy 4:11).

Christian tradition believes that Mark later worked in Rome and Alexandria—possibly founding the church in that city. He died as a martyr in Alexandria. His body was taken to Venice in the 9th century where his remains are venerated in St Mark's cathedral.

Date

Tradition suggests that Mark wrote his Gospel in Rome, soon after the death of Peter (about AD 65).

Language and style

Mark writes in a simple, popular Greek—the literary language of the Roman Empire. His sentence construction is poor, and he introduces strange Aramaic and Latin words, far more than the other Evangelists. This suggests that as a Jew he thought and spoke in Aramaic, though he could just about manage Greek as a foreign language, whilst living in a Roman environment. However if Mark's Greek is not very polished it does not detract from his colourful descriptive power. The language is that of everyday life.

Why did Mark write?

Mark wrote during deeply troubled times. Rome was burnt down in AD 64. Peter was crucified there in AD 65 and Paul beheaded in AD 67.

The Roman Emperor, Nero, committed suicide the following year leaving four rival generals fighting over the empty throne.

The Christians in Rome had been blamed for the destruction of the city, and many were martyred. Against this background of conflict and persecution, Mark collected some of the traditional stories about Jesus, and strung them together into a coherent narrative, to form an introduction to his account of Jesus' death on the cross. To be a follower of Jesus, he seems to say, means following that way of the cross, and being a martyr.

St Mark, after a Venice mosaic

A5 About the land

Palestine is a small, Middle-Eastern country, small enough to fit into the South of England between Kent and Devon. It is, in fact, only a narrow strip of land between the Mediterranean Sea and the desert which lies east of the River Jordan.

This river is its most prominent feature. It runs from north to south and is part of the great geological Rift Valley which stretches from Syria to Africa. The land here is well below sea-level. It is at its lowest point near Jericho on the Dead Sea, 395 metres below sea-level (1292 feet).

But Palestine is a land of great contrasts. The valley enjoys a tropical climate with exotic vegetation, yet within a short distance there is desert, and in some parts, mountains rising to over 1000 metres (3000+ feet).

Galilee in the north is a mountainous region, with windy moorlands around Nazareth. Yet the land quickly descends to the hot shores of Lake Galilee on the east, and the coastal plain on the west.

Jerusalem lies in the south, on the high land of the Judaean hills with its temperate climate. The short distance from Jerusalem to Jericho is a drop of over 925 metres (3000 feet).

The vast plain of Esdraelon divides Galilee from these southern hills. Extensive agriculture is possible here and on the coastal plain. The land enjoys a warmer and drier climate than other Mediterranean countries, but it yields similar produce.

Olives are the most important crop. They have been grown since biblical times, along with grapes and figs. Other fruits, such as citrus fruits (Jaffa oranges), bananas and avocado pears have only been introduced in recent years. There are also cereal crops of wheat and barley.

Careful distribution of water and modern agricultural progress has transformed some of the most inhospitable desert. Today, many people in Palestine work in community farms, called kibbutzim. They produce astonishing results from unpromising soil.

Yet even in biblical times the clever King Herod found a way of channelling the winter rain water into reservoirs. He was so successful that his desert palace on the mountain of Masada, near the Dead Sea, had its own swimming pool.

The following section lists all the places mentioned in Mark's Gospel.

The Palestine of Mark's Gospel

The Palestine of Mark's Gospel

Arimathea   The home of one of Jesus' friends (Mark 15:42). In the Old Testament it is known as Ramah, and lies north-west of Jerusalem.

Bethany ⎱   Two villages near Jerusalem, separated from the City by
Bethphage ⎰   the Mount of Olives.

Bethsaida   A fishing village on the north-eastern shore of Lake Galilee (Mark 6:45, 8:22). According to the Gospel of John it was the home of the disciples Peter, Andrew and Philip.

Caesarea Philippi   Herod's son Philip built a town at the source of the river Jordan and named it 'Caesartown' in honour of the Roman Emperor. It was the scene of an important event in Mark 8:27.

Capernaum   A town on the north-west shore of Lake Galilee, on the main through-road to Damascus. Close to the Galilee border, it was a busy frontier town and customs station (Levi the tax-collector became a disciple of Jesus there, Mark 2:14). Jesus seems to have chosen it as the headquarters of his ministry in Galilee. It is mentioned frequently in the Gospel.

Galilee   The most northerly of the three districts into which Palestine has been traditionally divided. With its varied scenery it remains today the most attractive part of the country, producing a healthy and hardworking race. It was from this hardy stock that Jesus was born and later chose his first disciples.

Gennesaret   A fertile plain on the west of Lake Galilee (Mark 6:53).

Gerasa   A town on the eastern shore of Lake Galilee, according to Mark 5:1. The famous Ten-Towns cities of Gerasa (Jerash) and Gadara are several kilometres distant, and Mark's reference may be to the recently discovered ruins of a small town called Kursi.

Idumea   The New Testament name for the land of the Edomites, in the south of Palestine, counted as part of Judea in the time of Jesus (see Mark 3:8). Herod the Great came from this country, and ruled Palestine when Jesus was born.

Jericho   A very old city, perhaps the oldest in the world. Situated in the Jordan valley, just north of the Dead Sea, it once guarded the eastern approach to Palestine. It is mentioned in the New Testament as one of the places where Jesus preached (Mark 10:46).

Jerusalem   The capital of Judaea. (See page 9.)

a   A Bedouin
b   The Sea of Galilee
c   Jerusalem

d

d *Part of Holy Sepulchre Church*
e *A market in the old Jerusalem*
f *St Peter's Church on the Galilee Sea*

e

f

Jordan Palestine's principal river is unnavigable and (until recent times) unprofitable. But it effectively divides Palestine from the lands to the east, even today. As such it played a star role at the end of the Exodus story, and so was the site chosen by John the Baptist for people to repeat the Exodus story by being baptized (Mark 1: 5).

Judaea means the land of the Jews, descendents of Judah, one of the twelve tribes of Israel. Its capital is Jerusalem. In the time of Jesus it was ruled, together with Samaria and Idumea by a governor appointed by Rome.

Lake Galilee A large freshwater lake in northern Palestine, 21 kilometres long and 12 kilometres wide, the scene of much of Jesus' ministry. Hemmed in by hills, it is susceptible to sudden storms (Mark 4: 37). It has been famous throughout history for its fish and it was among its fishermen that Jesus made his first disciples (Mark 1: 16).

Magdala The Galilean lakeside village home of Mary, one of the earliest followers of Jesus, prominent in the story of his death and resurrection (Mark 15: 40, 16: 1).

Nazareth A village in the hills of Galilee, the home of Jesus and his parents (Mark 1: 9). He seems to have left it early in his career to conduct his ministry in the lakeside towns.

Phoenicia A confederation of trading cities, operating from the sea coast north of Palestine, the modern Lebanon (Mark 7: 26).

Sidon An ancient Phoenician harbour, north of Tyre (Mark 3: 8, and 7: 31).

Ten-Towns The name given in Roman times (Decapolis) to the territory east of the Jordan, where ten famous cities formed a loose confederation (Mark 5: 20, 7: 31).

Tyre An ancient and important harbour on the coast of Phoenicia. (See Mark 3: 8, 7: 24).

A6 About the Jews

History

Jesus was a Jew. Mark was a Jew. The history of the Jewish people is complex. The following summary is inevitably over-simplified, but it provides some sort of background against which to read the Gospel of Mark.

3000 BC	Palestine inhabited by Hebrew-speaking Canaanites.
1800	Immigration of nomadic shepherds. Abraham, Isaac, Jacob (Israel). Some Israelites emigrate to Egypt.
1200	Israelites partially conquer Palestine under Joshua. Israelite 'Judges'—Samuel.
1050	Israelites adopt monarchy—Saul.
1000	David establishes Jerusalem as capital.
950	Solomon builds the First Temple.
930	The kingdom splits into two, Judah (south) and Israel (north).
721	Northern kingdom overrun by Assyrians. Permanent exile.
586	Southern kingdom overrun by Babylonians. Exile for 50 years.
538	Under Persian rule, Jewish (Judah) exiles return and build Second Temple.
332	Alexander the Great's Greek Empire stretches from Europe to India.
167	Maccabees win Jewish independence.
63	Greek Empire taken over by Rome.
37	Rome appoints Herod the Great as king of the Jews. Second Temple enlarged.
6	Jesus born.
AD 27	Public ministry of Jesus.
30	Jesus crucified.
65	Mark writes his Gospel.
66	Jews rise in revolt against Rome. Masada.
70	Jerusalem is destroyed by the Roman army. Temple is never rebuilt.

Those who originally divided the years into BC (before Christ) and AD (after Christ) mis-calculated the birth of Jesus by 6 years.

Language

Aramaic was the original language of the nomadic people from whom Abraham and the Israelites were descended. When the nomadic people entered Palestine they adopted *Hebrew*, the language of the Canaanite inhabitants. However, when the Jews were exiled to Babylonia (586 BC) they reverted to their original spoken Aramaic. They kept Hebrew as the sacred language for their worship and writings.

In 332 BC the country was conquered by Alexander the Great and *Greek* became the spoken language of the whole civilized world of that time. From then onwards many Jewish books were written in Greek. Jesus and Mark would have spoken Aramaic and possibly a popular Greek for conducting official business. They read the Jewish scriptures and worshipped in Hebrew. Mark wrote his Gospel in Greek.

The Jewish people

At the time of Jesus, Palestine was inhabited by various groups. In the southern province of Judaea lived the descendants of Jacob's son Judah, (the Jews), proud of their faithfulness to tradition. They tended to look down on the Jews who lived in the northern province of 'Galilee of the Gentiles' as it was called, who were suspected of intermarriage with non-Jewish stock. Jesus and most of his disciples came from Galilee. Between the two, the Samaritans were boycotted by both Northerners and Southerners because they were clearly a mongrel race, though they remained true to the religion of Abraham and Moses. The Arab peoples who lived in the lands south and east of Palestine also claimed descent from Abraham. They later conquered Palestine and ruled it from AD 640 to AD 1100. Their descendents share the land with Jews today.

1 Jewish life-style

Some Jews remained nomadic shepherds like their ancestors, travelling constantly to find pasture for their flocks in the stony 'desert' of Palestine. Many more farmed the land for crops. Some worked as fishermen on Lake Galilee, as many still do today. Jesus' first followers were fishermen.

A shepherd leading his flock

Villages and small towns like Nazareth were not deeply influenced by the Roman occupation. The houses were simple, built of baked mud. They were like boxes, their flat roofs made of branches and rough rafters which could easily be removed (Mark 2:4). The roofs were good places to ripen fruit, dry clothes, sleep and say prayers. The inside of the house was sometimes at two levels; living quarters for the family were on one level with the other being used for animals or as the family workshop. Jesus was a carpenter, who probably made furniture for his neighbours and mended their roofs. Perhaps he also repaired the fishermen's boats. (Was that how he got to know Peter and his friends? Mark 1:16.)

Larger towns, like Jerusalem, Samaria and Caesarea, were more Roman in style. Jerusalem boasted a stadium, theatres, streets with colonnades, baths and fine houses of stone or brick with shaded court-yards. The Romans had in fact, simply copied the Greek style. The Ten-Towns (Decapolis) mentioned in Mark 5:20, 7:31, were basically Greek cities.

Rich Jews in the cities tended to copy Roman behaviour. Others clung fiercely to their traditional Jewish customs and style.

From ancient mosaic pictures we know how they dressed. Ordinary people went barefoot or in sandals. Men wore a long, cotton shirt, usually belted and with a cloak over it. At prayer they covered their head with a prayer shawl, called a 'tallith'. Underneath it, they wore a skull cap, still the distinctive headwear of the Jews today.

Jewish women wore similar dress, but their long robe was usually embroidered, and instead of the tallith they wore a veil. Today's Bedouin women, who come in from the country to sell their goods in Jerusalem's market (suq), dress just like this.

2   Family life

The mother played a prominent role in family life, especially at the festival celebrations in the home. Family life was led in close obedience to the *Torah*, the Law of Moses. This included strict rules about diet. They had only two meals a day, at midday and evening. (Romans had four meals.) Meat was eaten only occasionally and had to be killed in a way which drained all the blood out. This was called 'kosher' or 'correct' meat. Garlic and onions spiced the raw vegetables. Olives were the staple diet, with cereals, nuts, dates and grapes. Milk and wine were drunk.

It was at home that the children learned most about their Jewish tradition and practices. An important family celebration was the Friday supper (Sabbath began on Friday evening at sunset) at which the mother presided.

3   Education

Literacy was high in Palestine. The Jewish boys attended good schools and regarded their teachers most highly. Girls received no schooling outside the home. From five or six years of age boys attended school in the synagogue where the teaching was entirely religious, with no such things as mathematics, music or physical education. The boys, who sat in a semi-circle on the floor, learned by a question and answer method. The older boys discussed theology and learned the Law of Moses.

A high point in a boy's life was his *Bar Mitzvah* (Son of the Law). At this celebration the adolescent boy received his 'tallith' and took up the adult privileges of the synagogue. On the following Sabbath he read the Law for the first time in the synagogue. It is still an important event in a Jewish boy's life today.

4   Jewish worship and festivals

Jerusalem, high in the Judaean hills was the stronghold of Jewish tradition. Jews streamed to its *Temple* at the time of their festivals. For Jerusalem was not simply the capital city, it was the Holy Mountain where God had chosen to enter into close communion with his people. Because of the Temple it was the City of God. It was only in the Temple that priests ministered and sacrifice was offered.

When the Jews were exiled in Babylonia in 586 BC, they set up meeting places for prayer and scripture reading. These were called *synagogues*. They brought this new-style worship back into Palestine, and eventually every local community had its own synagogue. Jesus was brought up on the synagogue service before he began to preach in the synagogue himself. (Mark 1:21, 3:1, 6:2, etc.)

The Western Wall of the Temple

The main *festivals* which were celebrated in the Temple, synagogues and Jewish homes (and are still celebrated by Jews today) are as follows:

Passover (Pesach): the spring commemoration of the Exodus from Egypt, which was seen as the event in which God 'chose' Israel (Mark 14:1, 12).

Pentecost (Weeks): the first Harvest Festival, fifty days later, marking the end of the Exodus journey.

Tabernacles (Sukkot): the autumn festival, when open-air 'tabernacles' or tents were put up while the harvest was gathered.

Atonement (Yom Kippur): a day of repentance for the year's sins, and of prayer for being again 'at one' with God.

Dedication (Hannukah): a winter feast of light commemorating the rededication of the Temple in Maccabee times (64 BC).

Purim: a late-winter children's feast, with fancy dress and presents.

A child celebrates Hannukah

An elderly man celebrates Sukkot

Religious groups in Mark

According to the Gospels, Jesus was frequently challenged for the religious views he held. But even the authorities of his time were not agreed amongst themselves. The groups and officials mentioned in Mark's Gospel in alphabetical order are:

1   Council (14:55, 15:1, 15:42)
The Council (Sanhedrin) was the parliament which ran the affairs of the Jewish nation at this time—in so far as the rule of Rome allowed it. It was composed of the chief priests, prominent Jerusalem laymen (elders) and the experts in Jewish Law.

2   Elders (14:43, 53; 15:1)
Prominent and respected laymen of Jerusalem.

3   Herod's Party (3:6, 8:15, 12:13)
This political party aimed to get rid of the Roman domination of Palestine by restoring the kingdom of the Herod family. The Herod dynasty existed for fifty years before Jesus until a hundred years after his death.

4   Pharisees (2:16, 18, 24; 3:6 etc.)
The Oxford Dictionary definition of 'Pharisee' is 'a self-righteous person, hypocrite'. Pharisees got this bad name because some of them were very critical of Jesus' teaching. But many others welcomed his message, since it echoed so strongly their own warm love of God. They were lay people who tried to become holy by keeping the Law of Moses in exact detail. Like Jesus, they were opposed to the professional holy people—the Sadducee priests—whom they thought too materialistic ever to find God.

5   Priests (14:1, 10, 43, 53)
When the Jews returned from Babylonian Exile about five hundred years before Christ, the leadership of the nation passed into the hands of the priests, who claimed descent from Aaron. The chief of these took on a kinglike role, as the supreme mediator between God and his people. In 170 BC the last of the hereditary High Priests was murdered, and the office went to the highest bidder. It caused revolution. By the time of Jesus the Chief Priest was a political figurehead, chosen by Rome from aristocratic Jerusalem Sadducees.

6   Sadducees (12:18)
Mark only once refers to this priestly party, but there is evidence in the Acts of the Apostles (4:1, 5:17 etc.) that they formed the chief opposition party to Jesus and his followers. They were the rich land owners and merchants. They only stayed in power by collaborating with the Greek and Roman governments respectively. Their religious ideas were very conservative.

7   Teacher (5:35, 9:38, 10:17, 51, 12:19, 14:45)
In these texts Jesus is addressed as 'Teacher' or 'Rabbi'. In modern times the rabbi is head of the Jewish community, but in the Gospel it was a courtesy title, like 'sir'.

8 Teachers of the Law (Scribes) (1:22, 2:6, 11:18, 12:38, 14:1, 15:31)

In ancient times only scholars could read and write. The Scribes or Jewish writers came into prominence during the Babylonian Exile (586 BC). With the Temple and monarchy gone, the sacred writings became very important. These Scribes not only collected, copied and edited the writings, but started to teach and interpret them. Jesus complained that they often misinterpreted them (see 12:38).

9 Zealots (3:18)

These were Jewish terrorists active in Palestine during and after the time of Jesus. Their motives (unlike those of the Herodians) were more religious than political. They aimed to rid the country of pagan Roman rule once and for all—even by using violence. From this unlikely group Jesus chose one of his close followers, Simon the Zealot (patriot).

A7 About the Romans

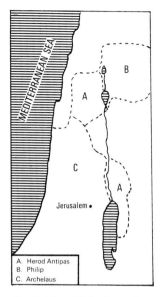

The division of Palestine under the Romans

A. Herod Antipas
B. Philip
C. Archelaus

Palestine was under Roman rule from 63 BC when Pompey took Jerusalem. It became part of the Roman province of Syria. Rome appointed Herod the Great as 'King' in 37 BC. When he died his 'kingdom' was divided among his three sons: Herod Antipas, Philip and Archelaus. The map shows their territories.

Archelaus was eventually deposed by Rome as he had been a cruel ruler. He was replaced by direct Roman rule in the form of a 'procurator' or 'governor'. From AD 26 to AD 36 this procurator was Pontius Pilate. (Mark 15:1.)

Rome had made the coastal town of *Caesarea* the new capital and put the main garrison of soldiers there. The lovely town on the sea was created by Herod the Great. He sunk thousands of cubic metres of stone into the sea to construct the artificial harbour. Visitors today are surprised as they swim in the bay to see Roman columns lying beneath the waves. The town had a palace, theatre, hippodrome and a temple dedicated to the Emperor Augustus.

The presence of soldiers was strongest in Jerusalem, where Herod the Great had built the Antonia fortress overlooking the Temple area. This was always a potential trouble spot.

A Roman camp seen from Masada

Most visitors to Israel today will visit Masada, the massive rock near the Dead Sea. Herod had built a superb palace there. After he died it became a Roman garrison, but was captured by the Zealots in the rebellion of AD 66. Here the Zealots made a brave last stand against the Romans before committing mass-suicide. The Roman army laid siege to it for five years. Remains of the army camps can still be seen.

Mt Masada towers over a small settlement at its foot

Readers of the Gospels cannot fail to notice the tension that existed between the Jewish people and the occupying forces. People who worked for the Romans were considered traitors or outcasts. It was a surprise to see Jesus choose a hated tax-collector, Levi, for one of his close disciples (Mark 2:14ff). The paying of tax to Rome was always a bone of contention (Mark 12:13ff).

Many Jewish people were waiting for someone to deliver them from Roman domination. Was it going to be Jesus?

Part B

─── Mark's Story ───

St Peter dictating the Gospel to St Mark

B1   Introduction

*Misericord from Norwich
Cathedral symbolizing Mark*

Visitors to St Mark's in Venice are shown the tomb of the saint, beneath
the high altar. The body of the Evangelist, who was martyred in
Alexandria, is thought to have been brought to Venice by merchants in
the 9th century AD. In the small piazza to the side of the great cathedral,
a granite pillar carries Mark's emblem, the winged lion. This symbol was
chosen to embody the opening lines of the Gospel—the voice of John the
Baptist roaring in the wilderness.

These opening verses of Mark's Gospel are very important. They set
the scene and give us a clue as to what is to follow. It is necessary to
understand the problem which faced the early Christians. Their background was Jewish and this meant that they had deep faith in only *one*
God. The Romans, around them, believed in many gods. The words of
Deuteronomy still spoke to Christian hearts:

> *The Lord—and the Lord alone—is our God. Love the Lord your God
> with all your heart, with all your soul, and with all your strength.*
>
> Deuteronomy 6:4–5

Where then were they to place Jesus? Whenever they thought about
him, they found themselves thinking about God. And whenever they
turned their minds to God they could not get Jesus out of their thoughts.
How were they to place Jesus? Clearly, he stood in a unique relationship
to God. But how?

Mark offers his explanation.

B2 Mark's prologue

The Way In

Well, she's always been running. I can remember how outstanding she was in her first school sports day, aged 5. She left the rest of her class at the starting line. Everyone was amazed at her speed. She was always running and never let her older brothers beat her. And of course, even at that early age she would stop everything to watch athletics on the television. You might say that she was born with plimsolls on.

May 1987

So speaks the proud father of a sixteen-year-old girl who has just broken the 60-metre sprint World Record. Compare this newspaper interview with an entry he made in a diary he kept when the children were small.

Susie is obsessed with the boys' lego. She builds houses and cars every bit as complicated as theirs. When she hasn't got lego pieces all over the floor she is busy getting flour all over the kitchen, or her bedroom in an unholy mess. She's such a busy person that she hasn't even time to watch much television. She loves the mornings at school and is writing her name, reading a few words and painting the funniest pictures. I think she is going to be artistic. She did well at her school sports day.

May 1976

In the newspaper article the father is remembering his daughter's early years in the light of what she has just achieved. He is writing with hindsight. He is naturally selective because the triumph of her world record is in the front of his mind.

It is quite a frequent technique in film-making too, to present the end of the story first—briefly. It leaves the audience in no doubt about the final outcome. The film director is saying, 'Here is what finally happened. Now follow with me the unfolding of the drama to understand *how* events led to this conclusion.'

And so it was with Mark. In the first 13 verses of the Gospel he sets the scene. He tells us exactly who Jesus is. He knows the end of the story. From then on his material is deliberately selected to unfold the drama.

It will be helpful to have an outline of the Gospel to show how Mark set out his story. We will refer to it frequently.

A Prologue 1:1–13; Jesus the *Messiah-Christ, Son of God*

B Galilean Ministry 1:13–8:30
ch 1   A summary of what Jesus did and said
ch 2–3   5 controversy stories
ch 4   Parables
ch 5–8   Miracle stories
   8:30   Peter acknowledges Jesus as *Messiah-Christ*

C To Jerusalem 8:31–13:37
ch 8, 9, 10   The Passion foretold ⎫
ch 9   The Transfiguration ⎬ on discipleship
ch 10   Journey to Jerusalem ⎭
ch 11–12   6 controversy stories
ch 13   Jesus foretells the end

D Death and Resurrection 14:1–16:8
ch 14   Last Supper
ch 15   Passion and Death
   15:39   The centurion acknowledges Jesus as *Son of God*
ch 16   Resurrection

Main Issues

General Introduction

Mark didn't set out to write a biography—a detailed account of the life of Jesus from birth to death. The materials for constructing such a life story simply did not exist, even in his time. Nor were his readers interested in having a mere biography, telling them who his mother was, or what kind of job he had, or what he thought about marriage or the Galilean fishing industry.

Mark's readers were concerned with quite a different problem. They were Christians, that is to say, people who had accepted that Jesus was the Messiah-Christ, the long-expected answer to Israel's prayers, the one who would bring about God's undisputed rule over the world, the Kingdom of God. They had no difficulty in accepting Jesus as the Christ: indeed they claimed he was still alive and active among them. Their difficulty was that the Kingdom of God was as remote as ever: the wordy promises of the Old Testament simply had not come about, as far as they could experience. On the contrary, being a Christian in Rome only meant being pushed around and persecuted. Where was the Rule of God? In what sense was Jesus the Messiah? Only in the future?

Mark writes to reassure them. Jesus is indeed the Messiah, the very Son of God. But to be a son of God in the kind of world we live in *means* being persecuted. Had they perhaps become followers of Jesus without appreciating what it involved? To be persecuted was proof they were genuine disciples of Jesus: it was when they got on famously with the world that they could start worrying!

In short to say Jesus is Son of God is easy. To accept it is difficult. To live out its implications is crucifying. In fact, it is a kind of *secret*, hidden from most people's eyes.

Last prayer in the Coliseum

The secret

Mark is very fond of this idea of secrecy. In his Gospel, from the very first chapter, Jesus keeps hiding his identity and forbidding those who know who he is to tell others (21 times). Consequently people keep misunderstanding him, including his own disciples (19 times). His words and actions keep arousing amazement, wonder, astonishment and fear (27 times).

> *A man with an evil spirit in him screamed . . . 'I know who you are—you are God's messenger!' Jesus ordered the spirit 'Be quiet, and come out of the man!' . . . The people were all so amazed that they started saying to one another, 'What is this? Is it some kind of new teaching?'*
> Mark 1: 23–27

You will find this theme of secrecy and surprise in Matthew and Luke too (though not in John). The remarkable thing is that, using Mark's Gospel as they do, they tone the theme down so that it is less obvious, and add no new examples of their own. The theme is distinctively Mark's.

The Prologue

The secrecy theme will begin with Jesus' public preaching in verse 14. But before he comes to that, Mark inserts a thirteen-verse prologue, which begins in a bold and clear statement of what Jesus means for him:

> *This is the Good News about Jesus Christ, the Son of God.*
> Mark 1: 1

The next twelve verses will open out this sentence, and set the scene for the story that follows. The Good News is about Jesus, who is the Messiah-Christ, God's Chosen One, the mighty one proclaimed by John the Baptist, the one anointed with God's Spirit, the Son of God who does battle with Satan.

In the story that follows after this prologue, Mark will never be as clear as this again. In fact no human voice will make these unambiguous claims for Jesus until the last page. It is as if the readers, although they have been let into the secret, must now join those who don't know the secret, to ask with them, 'Who is this?' Mark will suggest that they must not answer the question too quickly. If they do they may not grasp its full implication.

Looking Deeper

Mark's prologue deserves close attention. It falls into three short sections:

1 Jesus and John the Baptist   1:2-8
2 Jesus' Baptism   1:9-11
3 Jesus' Temptation   1:12-13

An icon of John the Baptist

1 Jesus and John the Baptist (Mark 1:2-8)

It is clear from other New Testament writings that John the Baptist was an important figure of his day. He was famous for his one-man campaign of baptizing all who would come to him, to prepare them for the coming of God's Kingdom. He was convinced it was at hand. He attracted many followers, though his popularity eventually declined while that of Jesus grew. The actual relationship between the two figures remains ambiguous.

Mark tells us little about the Baptist. According to Mark he has no importance in his own right. His only role is to announce the coming of Jesus as the one who would bring about God's rule on earth. The Baptist takes second place to Jesus.

The torch-bearer brings a message

Many Old Testament texts longed for the coming of God. Mark combines two of the texts, from Malachi 3:1 and Isaiah 40:3, which speak of that coming being prepared by a messenger in the desert. Once that messenger had proclaimed his message, God must be in the wings, ready to make his entrance. The reader is meant to see the coming of Jesus on to the scene as the coming of God. Mark even changes Malachi's text. 'I will send my messenger to prepare the way for *me*' becomes, 'I will send my messenger ahead of *you* (Jesus) to clear the way for *you*.' (Mark 1:2.)

The Malachi text had spoken of this desert messenger as a return of the prophet Elijah, the anointer of Kings who, according to legend, had been whisked into heaven without dying. Mark will later (9:11) speak of the Baptist as a second Elijah. Here (1:6) he simply alludes to the theme in dressing the Baptist in Elijah clothes, and feeding him with Elijah food (see 2 Kings 1:8).

Very simply, then, Mark has shown that the setting is right for the coming of God's Kingdom. To prepare themselves for that climax of history, the Baptist calls on people to turn away from 'sin' (strictly, to redirect their aim, so that they don't keep 'missing the mark'), and to be baptized in the Jordan. The crossing of the Jordan was the final stage in the Israelite Exodus from Egypt. Once that barrier had been crossed, people thought, God's Kingdom would be established in Palestine. This was far from the case, as they slowly began to discover. John the Baptist was inviting the people to repeat the Exodus experience all over again. They had to come out of the Jordan afresh, to allow God's Kingdom to come once and for all. Even non-Jews were invited, and they responded in great numbers (1:5). God's Kingdom was clearly something deeper than Jewishness.

Even so, says Mark, John's Jordan-baptism was only a symbol of the real thing. The real 'baptism'—being plunged into the very Spirit of God—was still to come. The closing verses of this section (7-8) emphasize this:

(a) The next person on the scene will be even greater (literally 'more powerful') than John.

(b) He will have higher rank: John is unworthy of performing even the task of a slave for Jesus.

(c) He will immerse people in the Spirit of God, not simply in water.

2 Jesus' Baptism (Mark 1: 9–11)

Mark has no stories to tell about Jesus' life before this episode: they occur only in Matthew and Luke. For Mark, Jesus comes on to the scene in verse 9, with the reader already totally aware of who he is (unlike the people in the story). What happens in this episode simply adds heaven's own confirmation to what Mark (through the mouth of the Baptist) has already told us.

To baptize someone means to drown him, to push him under water as if he was going to die. To come up again out of such an experience was meant to feel like beginning life all over again, as new. This is what the Baptist was asking people to do, to prepare themselves to welcome the Kingdom of God.

Jesus joins the crowd waiting to be baptized. Mark feels no embarrassment about recording this, as Matthew will do (see Matthew 3:14ff, as if Jesus didn't need to be baptized). For Mark, Jesus naturally stands alongside his fellow Jews to welcome the coming of God's Kingdom.

The story contains three elements. Each element is a statement about who Jesus is, not a description of something that could have been caught on film.

A baptism in the River Jordan today

    God's Heaven is opened,
    God's Spirit comes down,
    God's Voice is heard.

God's Heaven is opened
Jewish tradition told of a God who was once upon a time very active on behalf of his people—rescuing them in the Exodus, speaking to them through the prophets, bringing them back from Exile. But those times, it was felt, were no longer. The prophets had all died out, and God seemed silent and remote, shut away behind the solid barrier of the sky. A late Old Testament writer had dramatically cried out to God, *'Why don't you tear the sky apart and come down?'* (Isaiah 64:1.) Mark presents Jesus' baptism as the answer to such prayers: the barrier between God and the world had been torn down, and God was once again accessible, sending his Spirit and speaking to the world.

The baptism of Jesus, from a 17th century Greek icon

God's Spirit comes down

Ideas about the Spirit of God were similar. According to tradition, the Spirit had been active in the creation of the world (see Genesis 1:1) and throughout Israel's history. This was especially so in the lives of chosen individuals upon whom the Spirit had come down—the prophets. Since the death of the last of these prophets, the Spirit was thought to be absent, and would only return when God announced the coming of his Kingdom.

To say that the Spirit came down on Jesus is to claim that here and now God's Kingdom had come.

Why 'like a dove' (1:10)? Perhaps as an echo of the creation story in Genesis 1, where the Spirit of God was said to have 'brooded' over the waters, as a dove does over her young. Perhaps Mark saw Jesus, humbly accepting John's baptism in the waters of the Jordan, as the beginning of a new creation, a new start for the world.

God's Voice is heard

The voice of God himself, finally, confirms that the messianic times have come. The voice is apparently addressed to Jesus only—there is no suggestion that the Baptist or the crowds heard it. But Mark wants his readers to hear it, so that they should be in no doubt about an aspect of Jesus which everyone in the rest of the Gospel keeps misunderstanding: he is the Son of God.

'Son of God' is a title given to many in the Old Testament—Adam, good people, the whole people of Israel. But it was given especially to kings when oil was put on their heads as a sign of God's Spirit coming upon them. In Jesus' time there had been no kings for 500 years. Mark sees Jesus, full of God's Spirit, as the final king everyone had hoped for—the Messiah. Verse 11 is a quotation from the coronation song, 'God said to me, You are my son.' (Psalm 2:7.) Into this quotation Mark slips in a reference to another Old Testament scene:

> *The Lord says, Here is my servant...the one I have chosen* with whom I am pleased. *I have filled him with my Spirit.*
>
> Isaiah 42:1

The servant in the Isaiah text was to fulfil his task through suffering. 'This also you must know,' says Mark, even if the actors in the story of Jesus don't know.

'You are my Son'

3 Jesus' Temptation (Mark 1:12–13)

Our English word 'temptation' suggests being lured or enticed or attracted to do something wrong. In this scene, Jesus is not being 'tempted' in that sense. He is being tested. This is his trial of strength. The Spirit with which he is filled *makes him go* out (1:12) to join battle with Satan. The rule of Satan must be overcome if God's Rule is to come, and Jesus takes the offensive. As Son of God, it is the first thing he has to do.

The world was thought to be dominated by Satan, with a vast number of devils and demons under his command. They were thought to live in the desert, the haunt of wild animals harmful to humans. It is here therefore that Jesus' contest takes place, though he remains protected like the Psalmist by God's angels:

> *God will put his angels in charge of you to protect you wherever you go . . .*
> *You will trample down lions and snakes, fierce lions and poisonous snakes.*
>
> Psalm 91

So the final battle has been joined, the restoration of the world is at hand. The battle will continue throughout Jesus' life. Mark is therefore giving his readers another clue to the meaning of the story that follows. Indeed, the battle will continue throughout the life of anyone who wishes to follow Jesus. They all have to undergo the same test.

Summary of the Prologue

The first 13 verses of the Gospel are a key to the meaning of the rest. They are not to be taken as a random series of anecdotes about Jesus, but as vital information which readers will need if they are to understand what follows. The readers are here let in on the secret of who Jesus really is, so that like Mark they know the end of the story before they begin reading about the men and women who wonder who Jesus is.

Jesus is the fulfilment of God's plans for the world. He is the Messiah-Christ who brings about the Rule of God on earth. His relationship with God is that of a son to a father. He shows what it means to be a Son of God. In him the barrier between the world and God is broken down. God's Spirit is once again at work in the world to overthrow the rule of Satan.

The three sections are linked by their common background—the desert—and by the repeated references to God's Spirit. If there are few references to the Spirit in the rest of the Gospel it is not because Mark loses interest in the subject. He is satisfied that it has all been said on this first page of his writing.

God's Spirit is at work in Jesus. Full stop.

The desert is the symbolic setting for the battle against the forces of evil

A Short answers (Knowledge)

1   What does the word *Christ* mean?
2   Which prophet does Mark quote at the opening of his Gospel?
3   Who said *'Turn away from your sins and be baptized'*?
4   Which river runs through Palestine?
5   What did John wear?
6   What did John eat?
7   From what town did Jesus come?
8   At the baptism of Jesus what did the dove symbolize?
9   What did the voice from heaven say?
10   How long was Jesus in the desert when he was tempted by Satan?

B Longer answers (Knowledge & understanding)

1   Who was John the Baptist?
2   Describe the baptism of Jesus as recorded by Mark.
3   The 'Prologue' of Mark can be divided into three short sections. What are they?

C Essays (Understanding & evaluation)

1   What is Mark's 'secret'? How does he reveal its meaning in the opening verses of his Gospel?
2   What was the relationship between John the Baptist and Jesus? Refer to the events described in the opening of Mark's Gospel.
3   'Matthew and Luke make John the Baptist the centre of the action in the riverside baptism scene. Mark doesn't make John so important.' Comment.
4   The baptism of Jesus as described by Mark has three elements. What are they? Comment on each one.
5   What do *you* think the temptation or testing of Jesus in the desert was about?

D Things to do

1   Prepare a collage called 'Temptation' with reference to Mark 1:12, Luke 4:1–13 and today's world.
2   Have a class/group discussion about *baptism*. Produce the results of your discussion as a visual display under three headings:
    (a) What it is;
    (b) What it meant to Jesus;
    (c) What it means today.
3   Prepare a five-minute talk on John the Baptist. You could use slides and music—like *Prepare ye the way of the Lord* from Godspell. You may want to use material from the other Gospels.
4   An icon of John the Baptist, like the one below and on page 22 is prominent in an Orthodox church. If there is a church near you, invite someone from that tradition to talk to you about icons.

B3 Teaching in parables

The Way In

A religious studies teacher was visiting Mount Sinai. He got into conversation with a Greek monk. The Englishman described in some detail his views about the sad split between Eastern and Western churches 900 years ago, and his own hopes for ecumenism (working together). He asked the Greek monk what he thought about it. Without a word, the monk took a piece of paper from his pocket. He tore it in two. One piece he called 'The East' and placed it inside a breast pocket next to his heart. The other half he called 'The West'. This he tore in half, and in half again, and again, and again. The paper was in shreds. He tossed the 32 pieces into the air. They fluttered away, helplessly, in the breeze.

A group of Christians were discussing 'sin'. A Roman Catholic described her Church's traditional view on the difference between *mortal* and *venial* sins. 'Venial sins are the ordinary, everyday wrongdoings; the lies, the cheating, the unkindnesses that we all fail in. Mortal sin is much more serious. It is "deadly" because it is a deliberate turning away from God. It cuts the person right off from God.' The group asked a Russian Orthodox priest how *he* would describe the difference between venial and mortal sins. He thought for a moment. 'Two penitents went to a holy monk in the desert,' he said. 'One confessed to a single, terrible sin. The monk sent her into the desert to search for the heaviest stone she could manage and bring it back to his hut. The other confessed to numerous small failings. They counted them: 273. The monk told her to go and collect 273 small stones from the desert. She also returned with them. The monk then told both penitents to go back and replace the stones exactly where they had found them.'

The Greek monk and the Russian priest are Easterners. They reply to questions by telling stories or acting them out. It seems strange to us because we are Westerners and we are given wordy, logical and abstract explanations to the questions we ask. We think that stories are 'only for children'. They think stories speak louder than words.

Mark was an Easterner. His response to the question 'Who is Jesus?' was a series of vivid slide-like pictures of Jesus in action. His writing is in great contrast to Paul's. Paul, the Westerner, wrote his letters around the same time as Mark, some of them even earlier. But Paul's style is totally different. He was influenced by Greek learning—just as we are. His letters are theological writings, full of abstract ideas and logical arguments. They correspond much more to *our* style of writing or teaching.

Jesus was a Jew. He was an Easterner who would naturally use a story rather than a logical argument. The stories he told are called *parables*. Mark includes only a few in his Gospel. (Luke records many more.)

> *Again Jesus began to teach beside Lake Galilee. The crowd gathered round him was so large that he got into a boat and sat in it. The boat was out in the water, and the crowd stood on the shore at the water's edge. He used parables to teach them many things...*
>
> Mark 4:1–2

The age-old tradition of storytelling

Main Issues

The Gospel proper begins in Chapter 1, verse 14.

In the Prologue Mark has told us who he believes Jesus is. Now he starts to give us scenes from Jesus' ministry in Galilee. A New Testament scholar, Morna Hooker, writes:

> *And now the curtain falls, and we are among men and women who stumble around, wondering what is happening.*
>
> *The Message of Mark* Epworth Press 1983

Jesus began his ministry, it would seem, as a continuation of the work of John the Baptist. He only began his active preaching when the Baptist had been removed to prison. And the content of his preaching was the Kingdom of God.

> *After John had been put in prison, Jesus went to Galilee and preached the Good News from God. 'The right time has come,' he said, 'and the Kingdom of God is near! Turn away from your sins and believe the Good News!'*
>
> Mark 1:14–15

John the Baptist's message had been the same: to turn away from sin. According to Matthew, he also linked that with the conviction that the Kingdom of God was close at hand. But whereas John the Baptist had made that sound like Bad News, with the threat of judgment hanging over people's heads, for Jesus it is nothing but Good News, to be welcomed with joy.

The Kingdom

When Jesus preached about the Kingdom of God, what would his audience have understood? When we talk about a kingdom today, we imagine a territory which has borders, a government of some kind and institutions which keep the population in control. But the ancient world was not so structured, nor so stable. A king's territory extended only as far as his rule influenced people. So the king's rule was more important than the territory he occupied. When Jesus was preaching about the Kingdom of God he was talking about God's Rule over people.

The men and women who listened to Jesus would have been familiar with the Jewish literature which had developed in the two centuries before their time. The constant message of that literature was of the need for a drastic intervention by God into history, to establish his kingly rule. His Way would triumph and people would live in peace and harmony. This idea of the Kingdom is central to Jesus' preaching. 'The right time had come,' and this final act of God's salvation was now taking place in and through the ministry of Jesus. In fact, as Mark saw it, you could say 'Jesus *is* the Kingdom of God'.

Mark's understanding of the Kingdom
Mark places great emphasis on the Rule of God because he saw the world of men and women as being under the Rule of Satan. Not that he thought all people were devilish: he knew there were many good people around. But even their best efforts were foiled again and again, because again and again they were overcome by the misuse of money, prestige and power. Evil reigned supreme.

Earthly kingdoms have clear borders

For Mark the coming of Jesus was the liberating good news that now at last this will change. At last someone *stronger* than Satan had appeared (see Mark 3: 27), who would show conclusively that goodness is more powerful than evil. When people were filled with the same godly Spirit that inspired Jesus, the Rule of God would replace the Rule of Satan. Goodness would reign supreme. That was the Good News.

Preaching through Parable

Jesus preached about the Kingdom of God by using parables. In fact the parables are often referred to as the Parables of the Kingdom, because many of them begin with the words, '*The Kingdom of God is like this*' (as in Mark 4: 26).

Parables are stories. The word 'parable' means 'to compare like with like'. Jesus wasn't the first person to use parables. The rabbis were renowned story-tellers.

Using these comparison stories, Jesus described what God and his Kingdom were like. His contemporaries thought that the Kingdom of God would come in the future. 'No,' said Jesus, 'it is here and now.' They also thought that only a chosen few would enter the Kingdom. 'No,' said Jesus, 'it is for anyone who wants it.'

Parables are often read as if they were general exhortations to be generous, or honest, or prudent, or just. This trivializes them. Parables *challenge* the listener. They ask questions and offer an unexpectedly new way of looking at things. God's ways turn our values upside down. Jesus

used his stories (often humorous) to shake up people, to make them reflect deeply both on the nature of God and on their relationship to Him.

'Listen,' he says, 'if you have ears.'

Mark 4:9

Parables in Mark

In the middle of his main chapter on parables (chapter 4), Mark represents the disciples as asking Jesus for an explanation. Matthew even puts the question, 'Why do you use parables when you talk to the people?'

The question is odd. You might as well ask a teacher why he or she used the blackboard. But the answer is odder still:

> *You have been given the secret of the Kingdom of God. But the others, who are on the outside, hear all things by means of parables, so that, 'They may look and look, yet not see; they may listen and listen, yet not understand. For if they did, they would turn to God, and he would forgive them.'*

Mark 4:11–12

Jesus' answer is such a strange one that Matthew, using Mark's text, tones it down. Jesus hides his message, he says, not *in order to* blind people, but *because* people are blind (see Matthew 13:13).

Why does Mark have this stern view of the parables? There are three possible explanations:

1　The text is *factual*. Jesus did in fact deliberately make his teaching unintelligible, in order to punish people. Very few accept this as an explanation. If you don't want people to understand what you say, it's easier to say nothing than to confuse them. Nor does it tie in with the way other Jews used parables (always to illustrate and clarify), or with the way Jesus used parables elsewhere in the Gospels. Even in Mark, Jesus is surprised when people don't see the point. (See Mark 4:13.)

2　The text is *fictional*. Jesus used parables, as other rabbis did, to make his message clearer to the Jews. But few Jews followed him. This was such a scandal that the early Church invented the 'explanation' that Jesus' teaching was obscure, hidden from the many, and divulged only to the few.

3   The text is *theological*—Mark's own device to present once again the difficulty of understanding deeply who Jesus is. What Jesus demands of anyone who wants to follow him is not easily acceptable, or even easily understood. It needs reflection.

The parables he told were therefore a sort of touchstone, sorting out serious people from superficial ones. He was saying, 'Think about this. Do you realize the implications? To say that God's Rule is possible here and now will mean a revolution in your life.' Superficial people wouldn't see that. Serious people would.

In that sense, the parables *did* hide the truth from the hardhearted. There may even be a touch of frustrated irony in Mark's quotation of Isaiah: *'Go and preach the Word of God to people. It will only make them deafer and blinder! Otherwise they might be converted, and that wouldn't do at all!'* (See Isaiah 6:9–10.)

Even though Mark often speaks of Jesus as 'Teacher', his Gospel (compared with that of Matthew and Luke) contains few parables. Some of them are mere one-liners, a vivid metaphor to hit off the unexpected nature of God's Kingdom, in contrast to the skilful extended stories he is elsewhere said to have told. All of them, for Mark, are puzzling. He almost turns the word 'parable' into 'riddle'. Parables preserve the secret about Jesus for those in the know, and need Jesus' explanation before they will yield their secret.

Here is a full list of the long and short parables in Mark. The extended stories are asterisked (*).

The new patch will shrink and tear off some of the old cloth, making an even bigger hole.   (Mark 2:21)

The 17 Parables in Mark
The Kingdom of God is like: *Those unprepared for the Kingdom are like:*

Doctor healing the sick	2:17	Patched garment	2:21
Bridegroom and his guests	2:19	Old wineskins	2:22
Victory over divided Kingdom	3:23	Lamp under a bed	4:21
Victory over strong man	3:27	Savourless salt	9:49
*Abundant harvest (Sower)	4:3	*Murderous vinedressers	12:1
Lamp on a lampstand	4:21	Careless servant	13:36
A generous measure	4:25		
Seed growing secretly	4:26		
Mustard tree	4:30		
Flowering fig-tree	13:28		
Servants left in charge	13:33		

Looking Deeper

The Parable of the Sower (Mark 4: 3–20)

Understanding and interpreting the parables is more complicated than it may seem. We have to distinguish clearly between the original situation in which the parable was told, and the situation at the time it was retold in the Gospel. That is, between what the parable meant for Jesus, and what it meant for Mark writing more than thirty years later. The two are not necessarily the same.

The story itself is in verses 3–9: a farmer scatters his seed freely. Some gets wasted. Some doesn't produce a harvest. But the seed which does, more than compensates for the loss.

If the story is read on its own, without the 'explanation' offered in verses 13–20, it strikes an optimistic note. No farmer worries about the occasional seed lost in sowing—otherwise he'd never get a harvest at all. In spite of the loss, the harvest is quite out of proportion to the sowing—30, 60, or even 100 seeds for each one sown. That's why the farmer goes on sowing, prodigally. That's why there is always a harvest. God's Way is like that, says Jesus. He was challenging those who thought the Kingdom of God lay in the distant future. It doesn't. The harvest is always ready for reaping, here and now. The story is full of optimism, the Good News.

Why then is the 'explanation' so pessimistic, with its heavy concentration on the wasted seed? There is probably an echo here, not of Jesus' own time, but of the later Church for whom the Gospel was written. The second generation of Jesus' followers were beginning to encounter 'trouble and persecution' (verse 17), 'love for riches, and all other kinds of desires' (verse 19). The original enthusiasm was wearing thin, and many abandoned their Christianity. Jesus' parable is being reapplied to this new situation. This serves Mark's purpose well. Notice 'Satan' in verse 15. The Word of God is not understood by (does not 'bear fruit' in) everyone.

The reason scholars suggest that the 'explanation' in verses 13–20 comes not from Jesus but from the early Church is that it painstakingly spells out the details of the story, item by item. This makes the story into an *allegory*. Allegories are not usually used by preachers. They are difficult to construct if they are to remain consistent, and are more usually written rather than spoken. They need a 'key' before they reveal their meaning. Jesus' stories are simpler, taken straight from life, and are meant to make just one point, not a dozen.

But the Greek world loved the complexity of allegories, and the early Church grew up in that world. Many of the early Christian writers liked to treat the Gospel parables as allegories, and went into great detail 'explaining' them. It is unlikely that Jesus intended that to be done. He spoke as a poet, who leaves it to his listeners to discover their own interpretation.

It is probable that Mark thought of the other small parables in chapter 4 in the same cryptic way. For him, the true meaning of Jesus' preaching is like a Lamp that is at present hidden, to be made public only later (verse 21). It is like the Gift that is given to some and withheld from others (verse 25). It is like the Seed hidden in the soil, which will not come to light until harvest (verse 26). It is like the insignificant Mustard

Seed, which will eventually grow into a tree (verse 30).

But in their original context of Jesus' ministry, it is likely that these vivid images had a more optimistic meaning. The Good News is that God's Kingdom has been hidden by those who postpone it into the future. Jesus has come to fetch the Lamp from under the bed and put it up where it will enlighten everyone. The hidden Seed has already done its growing, and harvest time has come. The unpromising tiny Mustard Seed has already grown into a tree, and all the birds are invited to nest in its shade.

2   The Parable of the Vineyard (Tenants) (Mark 12:1–8)

Much of Mark's Gospel deals with the conflict between Jesus and his contemporaries (see page 56). In chapter 12 he presents Jesus as telling a developed parable on this theme, addressed deliberately at them. An absentee landlord farms out his vineyard to tenants. He sends agents to collect his rent. They are abused, and some are killed. So he sends his son. He is murdered. The tenants seize the property.

A typical incident in an occupied country fighting for independence. Jesus may have told the story of some recent nationalist unrest. He turns it into a question which forces his opponents to condemn themselves before they realize what they are saying. The landlord will confiscate the vineyard and give it to others. Israel was often spoken of as a vineyard (see Isaiah 5). Will the fact that it never produced the fruits expected of it lead to its condemnation? The same question had been put, even more dramatically, in the preceding chapter 11, where the Fig-tree (another image of Israel—see Jeremiah 8:13) is not ready with its fruit when the Messiah-Christ unexpectedly demands it.

It is again likely that the early Church added details to Jesus' story from life, to turn it into an allegory. As the parable now reads, it is clear to Mark's readers that the landlord stands for God, the successive agents stand for the Old Testament prophets, the 'own dear son' stands for Jesus (that is the title given him at the Baptism and Transfiguration), and the new tenants stand for the Christian Church. The stone which the builders reject as worthless will turn out to be the most important of all. The chapters which follow will tell of Jesus' death and resurrection.

3   Conclusion

Though Mark does not give us as many examples of Jesus' teaching as Matthew, Luke and John, he has many scenes in which Jesus appears teaching. He often refers to him as 'Teacher'. Much of Jesus' teaching would have been in parable form, as was customary among Jewish rabbis. All of the parables would have the same point: image after image to provoke his hearers, and make them reflect upon what God's Kingdom or Rule might involve. Could they see it coming about in Jesus' ministry, hidden though it was? Did they need to revise their ideas?

Mark has selected the examples of Jesus' teaching most relevant to his purpose. He wants to warn his readers that this teaching challenges them, as much as it challenged its first hearers.

A   Quick answers (Knowledge)

1   According to Mark what happened to John the Baptist before Jesus began to preach the Good News?

2   Name the first four disciples of Jesus.

3   What was their occupation?

4   How many parables are recorded by Mark?

5   According to Mark, Jesus gives a long explanation of one parable. Which one?

6   What happened when Jesus preached in the Nazareth synagogue?

7   To whom does Jesus address the parable of the Tenants in the Vineyard? (chapter 12)

8   To whom does Jesus address the parable of the Fig-tree and the Door-keeper? (chapter 13)

9   How did the Jewish leaders react to the parable?

10   What happened to the vineyard owner's son in the parable?

B   Longer answers (Knowledge & understanding)

1   What is a parable?

2   Make a list of the parables found in Mark that describe those unprepared for God's Kingdom.

3   What is an allegory?

4   Write a paragraph on the Kingdom.

C   Essays (Understanding & evaluation)

1   Tell in your own words the parable of the Sower. Why is it usually regarded as an allegory? What do biblical commentators say about this form of writing?

2   Describe in detail the parable of the Tenants in the Vineyard. Show how Jesus was directly confronting his enemies when he told the story. Do you think Mark adds anything in his telling of it?

3   Referring to some of the parables in the list on page 31, write an essay describing the Kingdom of God as Jesus saw it.

4   Comment on the parables in chapter 4 of Mark.

5   *'Understanding and interpreting the parables is not a straightforward exercise.'* Comment.

D   Things to do

1   Choose a parable. Find some appropriate music and pictures or slides to illustrate it. Give a five-minute presentation to your class/group.

2   The best-known parables are not found in Mark. They are in Luke. The Good Samaritan (Luke 10:25ff) and the Lost Son (Luke 15:11ff). Read them.

3   Make a collection of stories from the other religious traditions. Prepare a session where you present them to each other.

4   Write a parable to accompany this picture.

B4 Miracles

The Way In

When English cricketers are struggling against the powerful West Indians we are likely to hear the English Test Match Commentator say: 'Well, we need a *miracle* now to save the situation.' The 'miracle' required is probably a sudden thunderstorm. How many of the newspaper articles in the margin use the word 'miracle' in this way—nothing more than a surprising change of fortune?

Clearly Sam's headmaster meant something more than this when he said 'His recovery is definitely a miraculous answer to our prayers.' Some people would say that even this remarkable cure can be explained in medical terms. The doctors didn't actually say, 'But this simply *can't* happen.'

So what is it that makes something miraculous?

Is it simply the fact that people think it is?

Is it right to use the word to describe what is only extraordinary or unexpected?

Are some miracles events which are really quite natural? Or should the word strictly be used only for 'an event or action which violates the laws of nature'?

Ascension Day Mass for 'miracle' Sam

MANY happy returns: Same with mother Carol.

Spaniards told to expect no miracles

From Richard Wigg
Madrid

Make blind man see £10

Cataracts strike thousands of elderly people in India and Africa, leaving them blinded and helpless.

Yet cataracts can be cured by a simple operation that costs as little as £10.

Help the Aged is running ophthalmic programmes in India and Africa that are steadily eliminating as many cataracts as we have funds for – nearly 5000 last year. But our work cannot stop there.

Money is desperately needed to support projects that tackle the root causes of the problem – poverty, bad hygiene, malnutrition.

Please be as generous as you can, as soon as possible, because when blindness is the problem, prevention is the best cure of all.

To Help the Aged, Project 61716, FREEPOST, London EC1B 1BD.
I enclose my cheque/postal order for £
Name
Address
Postcode

Help the Aged

This baby died. Ten weeks later he was born! Anthony's heart stopped during a blood transfusion in the early months of his life in the womb. For three minutes doctors massaged his heart from outside the womb by pressing against his mother's stomach. Miraculously the little heart began beating again.

Main Issues

The newspaper cuttings show how we use the word 'miracle' in our everyday language. The miracle stories of the Gospels obviously refer to something more extraordinary than this. But what exactly were they? Scholars have argued long over that question.

It's important to realize that others apart from Jesus have been 'miracle workers'. The Old Testament is full of them. Indeed miracle stories feature in all the great religious traditions.

So Mark's description of Jesus' public ministry being accompanied, all the way through, by miracles is not surprising. Right from chapter 1 Jesus amazes the people not only by his preaching, but by the authority he shows in commanding an evil spirit to come out of a man. Preaching and performing miracles go hand in hand (Mark 1:21–28). The other Gospels present the same picture.

This does not mean that it is easy to know what Jesus actually did. Even when the Evangelists are clearly telling their readers the same story, they do not hesitate to include considerable differences. It would seem that the Gospel writers carefully selected only the stories which served their purpose. These they arranged and edited to make them illustrate their own themes. Take a look, for example, at the story of Jesus walking on the water as told by Mark (6:45ff) and retold by Matthew (14:22ff).

Mark's Gospel stands out for the space he devotes to Jesus' miracles. It is obvious that Mark considered the miracle stories as significant. So did the early believers who had handed down these stories to him.

For Mark the miracle stories bore witness to the power of God working in Jesus. The Rule of Satan was being replaced by the Rule of God.

The stories he selected for his Gospel can be put into groups. It will be helpful to look at them in these groupings.

Miracles in Mark

By his miracles Jesus showed that God's power was stronger:

1   *Than mental illness (demons)*
    Mark 1:23   Man with an evil spirit
          5:1   Man at Gerasa
          7:24   Daughter of the woman with faith
          9:14   Boy with an evil spirit

2   *Than physical illness*
    Mark 1:30   Peter's mother-in-law
          1:40   Man with skin disease
          2:1   Paralysed man
          3:1   Man with paralysed hand
          5:25   Woman with severe bleeding
          7:31   Deaf-mute*
          8:22   Blind man at Bethsaida*
          10:46   Blind Bartimaeus

3   *Than death*
    Mark 5:22   Jairus' daughter

4   *Than nature*
    Mark 4:35   Calming the storm
          6:31   Feeding of the thousands (5000)
          8:1   Feeding of the thousands (4000)
          6:45   Walking on the water

There are also several references to an unspecified number who were sick and possessed by demons.

Note   Miracles related only in Mark are marked with an asterisk.

Some Miracle Stories In More Detail

1   Mental illness

In New Testament times, much mental illness (psychiatric disorders, manic depression, paranoia etc) were thought to be the work of evil spirits living inside people. We have already noted that Mark starts the account of Jesus' ministry by describing how his teaching and activity were directed against these spirits. Verses 21–39 of the first chapter describe a number of events in quick succession where the authority of Jesus amazes the people. He drove out demons; he healed many who were sick; he preached in the synagogue. Mark wants us to see, here at the beginning of the ministry, that the Rule of Satan is giving way to the Rule of God. The evil spirits, (demons) are being destroyed by the Spirit of God at work in Jesus. The same power is shown in the authority with which Jesus preaches.

The man at Gerasa (Mark 5:1)

This is a strange story. It has all the features of other exorcism narratives. The suffering of the man is described in detail; the spirits recognize Jesus at once; Jesus commands them to come out; the pigs are destroyed to prove that the cure was achieved; the crowd are amazed.

The story contains some interesting further details.

1   The man believes he is possessed by a *legion* of evil spirits. A Roman Legion consisted of over 6000 men. Mark describes the man's massive strength. 'He was too strong for anyone to control him' (verse 4). But Jesus is stronger and overcomes not one spirit but thousands. The Kingdom of Satan has met with the Kingdom of God. The people are afraid when they see the extraordinary sight of the man, calm, clothed and in his right mind. The Spirit inspiring Jesus is more awesome than the spirit that had turned the man mad.

2   The request of the man to Jesus is strange. 'He kept begging Jesus not to send the evil spirits out of the region' (verse 10). The spirits themselves ask to be sent into a herd of pigs. That is what Jesus does, and the stampeding animals charge into the sea. No doubt Mark thought it better for the expelled spirits to enter unclean animals than other human beings. (He presumed they needed another home.) And as the Jews feared the sea, which they saw as a powerful beast, it would seem to be the best place to swallow up the herd.

3   The end of the story is important. The man, naturally, wants to go along with Jesus, his new friend. But Jesus asks him to stay behind amongst those who have treated him so badly, in order to preach to them. Mark takes every opportunity to remind us that what Jesus asks of any follower is not easy.

This is the first time in the Gospel that Jesus has been in Gentile territory. The story implies that the land is cleansed and therefore ready to receive Jesus. The man is sent to preach the Good News there. The story may have been intended to explain how this Gentile area became a home of Christianity very early on.

But what really happened?

Today we have psychological words to explain such cures. Many believe that this vivid story describes a crazy, sick man, who was made worse by the attitude of the people, who chained him up and made him an outcast. Perhaps his frantic behaviour frightened the swine, who stampeded to their death. We don't know how Jesus calmed such a sick person. It could be said that he was a good psychologist centuries before that science was practised. Is that the miracle?

The boy with an evil spirit (Mark 9:14)

This is the final exorcism story in the Gospel. It is complicated and may be made up of more than one original story. It seems to have been placed in this part of the Gospel because it emphasizes the necessity of faith.

In the story, the conversation takes place between Jesus and the child's father, because the boy is dumb. Jesus can cast out the evil spirit because of his own faith. The disciples cannot cast it out because of their lack of faith. Faith is demonstrated in this case by prayer. The disciples are like the father of the boy, still not wholly committed. 'I do have faith, but not enough.'

But what really happened?
Perhaps the boy had epilepsy, a disease understood today but attributed, in earlier days, to evil spirits. Jesus, bound by his own times, had never heard of epilepsy. In this story he shows the human impatience of someone frustrated by the situation and the inability of the disciples to deal with it.

Clearly something extraordinary happened through the presence of Jesus, but we will never know the details. Nevertheless we can perhaps understand why Mark included this narrative.

1   It follows the scene on the mountain where the disciples are very slow to understand the meaning of the transfiguration they have just witnessed (see page 49). This shows a lack of faith.

The immunisation programme is like a miracle to this lady

2   The last two verses speak of the importance of prayer for the exorcism of evil spirits. This could be a later addition to the story. The early Church may have been having difficulty in accounting for failure in the practice of exorcism.

3 Some scholars see parallels, in structure and language, between Mark's version of the story and John's later account of the raising of Lazarus (John 11). John's story seems to have later references to early Christian baptism. Community, prayer, faith, exorcism are all echoes of the early rite of baptism.

Miracles and Faith

The Gospel writers often point out that Jesus could only work miracles when the people had faith. Look at the story of the girl who was exorcised in Mark 7: 24. Jesus is reluctant to help but he is compelled to do so because of the extraordinary faith of this Gentile woman. Mark is stressing that miracles are not simply wonders to be marvelled at. They are *signs* of the presence of the Kingdom of God. People who understand who Jesus is (have faith) are already in touch with the Kingdom of God. In their case all things are possible. All evils can be overcome.

2 Physical illness

The miracles which describe restoration to physical health are not unlike the exorcism miracles. All physical disorders were regarded as forces which must be cast out of the body, like the demonic spirits. The Kingdom of God required their overthrow, because sickness kept people in bondage. Nature had been hijacked when limbs did not function and the human body was wasting away. It was controlled by evil forces, which did not allow people to achieve their full potential.

Paralysed man (Mark 2: 1)

This is the first of five consecutive stories of *conflict* between Jesus and the authorities. (See page 58.) The original story is told in verses 1–5 and 11–12 — a straightforward account of the dramatic healing of a paralysed man.

The story is interrupted in the middle by a conflict between Jesus and the authorities. It seems to reflect the early Church's concern with the forgiveness of sins.

Jewish tradition saw an intimate connection between sin and physical suffering. Suffering came only to the sinful. Jesus saw no connection. In this story he cures the paralytic to show that God wants him to be free of his disability. That being so, he proclaims that God does not hold people's sins against them.

By introducing the conflict Mark was expressing two things:
1 His theme of conflict whereby the authorities refused to see who Jesus really was. Here he implies that they had no excuse. The cure of the man should have convinced them he was God's agent.
2 The concern of the early Church to base its claim to minister to sinners on the authority of Jesus. Jesus proclaimed that sinners were forgiven because he spoke on behalf of God.

Man with a paralysed hand (Mark 3: 1–6)

This is the fifth of the stories of conflict between Jesus and the authorities. By this time the conflict leads to a plot to kill Jesus. The authorities are getting tired of being the losers.

It is by now taken for granted that Jesus can cure the sick. So the Pharisees set a trap to catch Jesus out. It backfires. It was the Sabbath, the day when Jews mustn't do unnecessary work. The authorities watch closely to see if Jesus will cure the man with the paralysed arm. He does so without hesitation, and defends his action by asking whether he should 'help' or 'harm', 'save a life or destroy it'. They can't answer.

Commentators suggest:

1   Mark is showing that concern for people is more important than laws. Exceptions must always be allowed.
2   Mark is again showing how the authorities are blind to who Jesus really is. (They themselves were, in fact, prepared to work on the Sabbath to save life. This man's life was not in danger. Why couldn't the cure wait until tomorrow?) Is Mark showing that Jesus had to work quickly because God's final battle against evil had begun? It couldn't be delayed. The real issue behind the miracle is the Pharisees' failure to understand this.

The blind man at Bethsaida (Mark 8:22)

This miracle story is found only in Mark. It is remarkably similar to the deaf-mute story (Mark 7:31) which is also found only in Mark. Both stories are different from others in the Gospel. In both Jesus is represented as using spittle. There are similar healing stories in Greek literature. Each story follows a 'feeding' miracle story. This seems to be intentional. (See page 44.) Neither story mentions evil possession or the need for faith. Each time Jesus requires silence about what has happened.

The story of the blind man is further distinguished by speaking of a cure taking place in two stages. Mark seems to have placed the story very carefully. The first stage of Jesus' ministry is over (Mark 1:16–8:26). When this story concludes it gives way to a second stage (Mark 8:27–10:52), where Jesus will gradually 'open the eyes' of the disciples about who he is. In this sense the story is a kind of parable. The man in the miracle story 'saw everything clearly'. In the next scene of the Gospel, Peter is going to pronounce 'You are the Messiah'. Mark is saying that Peter slowly 'saw everything clearly'.

Blind Bartimaeus (Mark 10:46)

This is the last healing story in the Gospel, and also seems to have been placed with great care at this point of the narrative.

The road from Jericho to Jerusalem is a long, hard one

Jesus is on his way to Jerusalem for the final conflict. The miracle takes place at Jericho, about 15 miles away. As Jericho is down at the Dead Sea, the climb up to Jerusalem would be a long and demanding one. The next section of the Gospel will be one in which things must be made absolutely clear. Here therefore, Mark presents the first public, unrebuked recognition of Jesus as Messiah. The secret has leaked out, and Jesus is hailed as Son of David by the blind beggar. Jesus cures him, and so acknowledges the title. Nor does he forbid the man to speak of what has happened.

This miracle story differs from others in focussing more attention on the blind man than on Jesus. It suggests that the story was used by the early Church to hold up this man as an example of discipleship. Here was a blind man who 'saw' that Jesus was the Son of David. What a contrast to the 'blindness' of disciples who had normal eyesight but who failed to understand.

The man was blind and helpless until Jesus opened his eyes. This is true of all people, says Mark. Although he is discouraged by others, his faith makes him determined. He is called, he responds immediately, and so he is saved. He then follows Jesus. Mark suggests that he follows Jesus to Jerusalem and straight into suffering. That is the kind of demand the Gospel makes on its readers.

Looking Deeper

Most of the miracles in Mark are miracles of healing. The '*nature miracles*' have always been more difficult to understand. Before we look at them in more detail we will have a brief look at how miracles have been understood over the centuries.

For centuries Christians never asked many questions about the miracles. They took the stories at face value. Some still do.

But in recent times some people have been more sceptical, Christians among them. Do things like this really happen? Did the Gospel writers mean these stories to be taken so literally. Would it not turn Jesus into a kind of magician? Are the stories simply legends which have later been attached to Jesus?

In taking the stories literally, Christians were using the definition of *miracle* referred to on page 35: 'An event or action which violates the laws of nature.' Since miracles were beyond the powers of nature, they were supernatural. They proved that the person who performed them was divine. The Roman Catholic Council of Bishops (Vatican I, 1870) even solemnly declared that this is what the Gospel miracles were about.

In fact, the definition of *miracles* as a violation of nature only grew up in the 18th century. Before then, nature and God were not so rigidly separated. People saw the miraculous wherever God's presence was felt. St Augustine of Hippo (died AD 430) said that the multiplication of corn in a cornfield was just as much a miracle as the multiplication of loaves in the desert. God was feeding people in both cases.

In the New Testament three Greek words are used for miracles, *teras*, *semeion* and *dynamis*.

1   *Teras* means *wonder*, something to marvel at.
2   This word is usually linked with *semeion*, which means a *significant event*. It is like a signpost, pointing to a deeper meaning.
3   The word used most often is *dynamis*. It means a work of *power*. In Jesus' actions the power of God is at work, and this is always power to save. No miracle ever fetches a rabbit out of a hat.

None of these Greek words suggest that Jesus violated any fixed laws of nature when he performed miracles. Indeed neither he nor his audience thought of nature as having fixed laws. 'Miracles occur at the edge of the possible' says a modern theologian (Gregory Baum *Man Becoming*).

Modern scholars

1   Modern scholars do not want to remove the miracles from the Gospels. They take them seriously. Professor Barclay says: 'They are not tall stories, but deep stories.'
2   It is quite clear that Jesus performed marvels. The stories are part of the fabric of the Gospel. Eliminate them from the Gospel and there is no Gospel left. He is even said to have told his disciples that they could do even greater things. (See John 14:12.)
3   This does not mean that no questions can be asked about the stories. Given the way the Gospels were put together, it is no longer possible to put our finger on the actual historical original event, only on what the early Christians made of it. When they saw marvels, they didn't ask, 'Can these sort of things happen?' but, 'What do they mean?'
4   What all the Gospel miracle stories mean is the death and resurrection of Jesus. The Gospels were written in retrospect, from the viewpoint of Easter Resurrection. All Jesus' miracles, as now told in the Gospels, are meant to evoke the risen Lord. The Christian reader is asked, 'Does Christ still work these kind of wonders for you?'
5   It is for this reason that the Gospels place such emphasis on *faith*: the faith of the readers, as well as the faith of those who first saw Jesus at work. For those who believe in God, and in Jesus as God's representative, no explanation is required. For unbelievers, no explanation is possible.

For the Christian, Jesus is no semi-divine wonder-worker. He is a man so completely one with the Father that in him and through him no limit can be set to the power of the Spirit of God. And that, he promises, goes also for all who allow that same Spirit to flood and control their lives.
J A Robinson *But That I Can't Believe*

A closer look at some of the nature miracle stories

Mark told these stories too with hindsight and in retrospect. Here, even more than in the other stories, it will be impossible to know 'what really happened'. We will look at possible explanations and try to discover what the stories meant to Mark and his readers.

Calming the storm (Mark 4: 35)

This story is like an exorcism miracle story. Since the sea was generally thought of as the chaotic home for evil spirits, this is understandable. Jesus commands the sea and the wind with the same words he had used in speaking to demons. (Compare 4: 39 with 1: 25.) So the whole story becomes a sort of parable. Jesus has come to still the chaos of Satan's reign.

The story concludes with the amazed disciples asking 'Who is this man? Even the wind and the waves obey him.' Mark offers no answer here. But his readers know the answer. They would perhaps remember Old Testament stories like the one in the Psalms:

> *The ships were lifted high in the air*
> *and plunged down into the depths.*
> *In such danger the men lost their courage; . . .*
> *Then in their trouble they called to the Lord,*
> *And he saved them from their distress.*
> *He calmed the raging storm,*
> *And the waves became quiet.*
>   Psalm 107: 26–29

Some commentators think the story could have been written to give heart to the early Church, suffering persecution. Mark would be pointing out that it is all very well revelling in the presence of Jesus when the sea is calm and the sky blue. A Christian must have faith even when all is in chaos. The early Christians were very ready to make allegories of the miracle stories (as of Jesus' parables) and apply them to their own situation.

D

The feeding of the five thousand (Mark 6:31)
The feeding of the four thousand (Mark 8:1)

The two stories are so similar that they may be versions of the same story. But Mark hasn't repeated himself by accident. The stories are very carefully placed in his narrative. In each, Jesus provides food for the crowd, and the disciples fail to understand its significance. So each story is followed by another miracle which is meant to leave them in no doubt.

1 The feeding of the 5000 leads on to the walking on the water story, and this concludes with the words, 'The disciples were completely amazed, because they had not understood the real meaning of the feeding of the 5000.'

2 The feeding of the 4000 leads on to a discussion about the miracle (which concludes, 'And you still don't understand?') and then to the miracle of the blind man at Bethsaida.

Some commentators see a link between the repeated feedings and the Old Testament story of God feeding his people over and over again in the desert. Others think that Mark tells two separate stories to show that both the Jews and the Gentiles are offered salvation.

The story of the feeding of the crowds is the only one recorded in all four Gospels. It is worth comparing the texts. (Mark 6:31, Matthew 14:13, Luke 9:10, John 6:1.)

It is interesting to notice the differences. Luke, for example, softens the story a little. His disciples sound less irritable. (Luke often does this to Mark's narrative.) John makes it an occasion for a long discussion on the Eucharist.

There are various ways in which this story could have arisen.

1 It could be a literal description of what happened. Jesus actually produced a vast amount of bread out of a few sandwiches.

2 Or maybe the people were so absorbed by Jesus' preaching that they barely nibbled at their food. A small amount went a long way.

3   Or perhaps it is just a parable commentary on the marvel of community sharing? Perhaps the crowd really did share, just as a group of young people might share their food at a pop concert. John Robinson tells how some friends of his once decided to put the theory into practice. They found that it worked. Robinson says, 'That hillside must have been a riot of conversation and laughter two thousand years ago.' (*But That I Can't Believe.*)

4   Or could it just be an exaggerated story? In reality the crowd was only a few hundred strong, and the food supply rather larger than stated.

5   Jesus knew of a secret store of food in a cave in the desert. He helped himself from it!

6   C H Dodd offered a political interpretation. The crowd was pro-Zealot, wanting to persuade Jesus to lead them in their fight against Rome. Jesus refused. The Kingdom was not like that. To show what it *was* like, he invited them to a symbolic sharing of a little bread. The Kingdom comes when people share together. The earliest account of the event (Mark's) concludes with the disciples being *amazed* because they didn't understand. Dodd thinks this wording was later misinterpreted to suggest that something extraordinary had occurred, when it hadn't.

7   The story could be entirely symbolic, with no historical basis. It is not unlike the Elisha story in 2 Kings 4:42–44. The Gospel writers would simply be reflecting on the Old Testament expectation of a Messianic Banquet, and on the eucharistic practices of the early Church. According to Mark the actions of Jesus are exactly the same as his actions at the Last Supper. Compare Mark 6:41, 8:6 and 14:22. Notice how in each case, Jesus took bread, gave thanks, broke the bread and gave it to his disciples.

Conclusion

What do you think of these theories? Some Christians are unhappy about the explanations which 'explain the miracle away'. They want a miracle to be a miracle. If all the sense of mystery is lost, what happens to the uniqueness of Jesus?

Other Christians accept that the actual historical facts are now lost to us. There is no answer to the question 'What really happened?', only to the question 'What did the story mean to Mark?' And what did it mean?

From what we now know of Mark it is becoming clear that he uses miracle stories to illustrate his conviction that Jesus was the one sent by God. He was sent to bring salvation to the Jews, indeed to the whole world. The hopes of the Old Testament have been fulfilled, and the Messianic Banquet is being shared out by Jesus, the host. For Mark the feeding story is about the fulness of life which is found in the Kingdom of God. It is important to remember that Mark is telling this story to people who already believe in a Jesus risen from the dead, and still present with them.

A Quick answers (Knowledge)

1 What miracle story is set in the territory of Gerasa?

2 What reply did Jesus give to the man who cried out, 'If you want to you can make me clean'?

3 How was the paralysed man brought to Jesus by four companions?

4 Where was Jesus when he cured the man with the paralysed hand?

5 Who said 'If I just touch his clothes, I will get well'?

6 What happened to Jairus' daughter?

7 What does 'Ephphatha' mean?

8 How many loaves of bread were shared by the 4000?

9 Who was Bartimaeus?

10 Which miracle stories are found only in Mark?

B Longer answers (Knowledge & understanding)

1 Describe the four categories into which the miracle stories are divided. Give examples.

2 In how many of the 16 miracle stories mentioned in Mark does the need for *faith* appear?

3 Describe in your own words the story of the man from Gerasa, who was possessed by demons.

4 Describe a miracle that concludes with Jesus in conflict with the authorities.

C Essays (Understanding & evaluation)

1 Choose two miracle stories, one where Jesus is seen showing God's power over nature, and one where he exercises God's power over death. Describe these events and comment on the reasons why Jesus is said to have performed the miracles.

2 Describe what happened in the stories of Jesus healing (a) a young boy or girl and (b) a man suffering from leprosy or blindness. Did faith have any part in these stories?

3 *'I can understand why Jesus would cure the sick. But why should he want to calm a storm? And did he really do it anyway?'* Comment, using some of the miracle stories told by Mark.

4 Comment on the Argus poster: *'Miracles happen only to those who believe in them.'* Did Jesus only work miracles for those who believed in them?

5 Describe the healing of blind Bartimaeus. Comment on the position of this miracle story in Mark's narrative. In what way is it a story about discipleship?

6 Mark has two stories of the feeding of the multitude. Why does he have the story twice? In what ways might these stories have arisen?

D Things to do

1 Make a display of pictures which depict the miracle stories in Mark's Gospel. As far as possible use contemporary material from magazines etc.

2 Look for miracle stories in the other religious traditions: (Jewish, Islamic, Hindu, Buddhist, Greek and Roman mythology). Make a collection and compare them with the miracle stories in the Gospels.

3 There are 16 miracle stories in Mark's Gospel (counting the two feeding miracles as one). See the list on page 36. Make a mural of the miracles by illustrating these 16 stories (collage, paintings, drawings or photographs). Use 16 sheets of card or paper and display (4 × 4).

4 *'Miracles still happen.'* Collect stories of modern miraculous cures or happenings.

B5 Watersheds

The Way In

In his autobiography *Is That It?* Bob Geldof starts with a delightful picture of his early life. Chapter 1 starts: 'Frank Lahiffe loved Mary O'Dwyer as well.' Bob and Frank were distracted in class by Mary, who sat between them. They were all four years old!

But the reason for writing his story is on page 215, where the pop singer describes the evening that changed the direction of his life. Chapter 13 starts:

> *All day long I had been on the phone trying desperately to get something happening with the single. It was coming to the end of 1984 and I could see no prospect for the release of* 'In the Long Grass', *which we'd sweated over and were proud of. I went home in a state of blank resignation and switched on the television. I saw something that placed my worries in a ghastly new perspective. The news report was of famine in Ethiopia . . .*
>
> Bob Geldof *Is That It?* Sidgwick and Jackson 1986

That half-hour of television viewing altered his life profoundly. The pop star of Boomtown Rats became the spokesman for the starving of Africa. We could call the programme on Ethiopia 'a watershed' in Bob Geldof's life.

What is a watershed? Geographically it is the line of separation on high ground where rainfall begins to flow in a different direction.

Most adults see some event in their lives as decisive. It remains etched on their memory. It may indeed, have altered the direction of their lives. For some it may have been a chance meeting, for others a failed examination. For Metropolitan Anthony (Bloom), the leader of the Russian Orthodox Church in England, it was the reading of Mark's Gospel that changed his life.

One day—it was during Lent, and I was then a member of one of the Russian youth organizations in Paris—one of the leaders came up to me and said, 'We have invited a priest to talk to you, come.' I answered with violent indignation that I would not. I had no use for the Church. I did not believe in God. I did not want to waste any of my time . . .

'Don't listen' the leader said, 'I don't care, but just sit and be a physical presence.' That much loyalty I was prepared to give my youth organization, so I sat through the lecture. I didn't intend to listen. But my ears pricked up. I became more and more indignant. I saw a vision of Christ and Christianity that was profoundly repulsive to me. When the lecture was over I hurried home in order to check the truth of what he had been saying. I asked my mother whether she had a book of the Gospel, because I wanted to know whether the Gospel would support the monstrous impression I had derived from his talk. I expected nothing good from my reading, so I counted the chapters of the four Gospels to be sure I read the shortest, not to waste time unnecessarily. I started to read St Mark's Gospel.

While I was reading the beginning of St Mark's Gospel, before I reached the third chapter, I suddenly became aware that on the other side of my desk there was a presence. And the certainty was so strong that it was Christ standing there that it has never left me. This was the real *turning point.*

Anthony Bloom *School for Prayer* DLT *1970*

Main Issues

Chapter 8 is a turning point in the Gospel. A watershed. The disciples learn who Jesus is. Jesus begins to speak of his suffering and death. From this point in the Gospel Jesus starts on his journey to Jerusalem and the cross.

The disciples learn who Jesus is

We have already looked at the first part of chapter 8. Jesus feeds the hungry multitude. But the disciples don't understand what it means (Mark 8:21). They are like the blind man at Bethsaida. They only learn in stages to see the truth about Jesus (Mark 8:22–26).

The scene described by Mark in verses 27–30 is a very important one in the Gospel. Jesus takes his disciples north to Caesarea Philippi. People are talking about Jesus by now and he asks his friends what they are saying. *'Tell me, who do people say I am?'* They reply that some think he must be John the Baptist returned, or Elijah or one of the prophets. Jesus pushes them further. *'Who do you say I am?'* Peter replies, *'You are the Messiah-Christ.'* The secret is out, Peter has found the right description of Jesus. He is the awaited one, the bringer of salvation from God.

Mark's account of the incident is very short, and it implies that Jesus accepts this description of himself. But he orders them to keep quiet about it. Why? Because in actual fact he never personally claimed the title? Or because he felt the title would be misleading (to Jews it meant a political military leader)? Or because *Mark* doesn't want the title blurted out too soon, without realizing it involves the cross? (See page 87.) Certainly Peter gets it wrong in the next verse.

Jesus predicts his suffering and death

To make it clear to Peter and the disciples that he sees his task quite differently from the general expectations, Jesus immediately predicts his suffering and death (verses 31–33). Peter doesn't like that at all, and protests. Jesus rebukes him for still not fully understanding. He even calls him Satan. The disciples would prefer a successful, victorious, glorious Messiah. Jesus needs to teach his followers that to be God's representative in our sort of world means martyrdom.

The verses contained in 8:34–9:1 were probably added by Mark to reinforce this teaching. Jesus challenges his disciples. They have shared his ministry of healing and preaching in Galilee; now they have to be prepared to share his final fate. 'If anyone wants to come with me, he must forget self, carry his cross, and follow me.' This is one of the few sayings of Jesus included in all four Gospels. It was therefore a very well-known and well-used saying in the early Church. Taking up a cross was a vivid and painful image of execution for people of the 1st century. Luke toned down its sharpness by adding 'daily'. It has been toned down even further by its constant repetition over the centuries.

Young people carry a cross through Norwich, with their bishop

Other predictions of suffering and death

1 Mark 9:30–32. Jesus speaks of being handed over to men who will kill him. But he will rise to life in three days. The disciples don't understand.
2 Mark 10:32–34. Jesus, now on the road to Jerusalem, tells his disciples that he is going to be handed over to the chief priests and teachers of the Law. He will be badly treated, killed and then three days later will rise to life. The disciples are terrified.

The threefold repetition of this prediction reinforces Mark's understanding of Jesus' task. No one can tell to what extent Jesus would have been able to make such accurate predictions.

The Transfiguration (Mark 9:2–13)

Peter has just declared that Jesus is the Messiah. Jesus has replied by saying this will involve suffering. The disciples are bewildered by the suggestion. In this context Mark introduces the story of the Transfiguration. Jesus and three disciples go up a mountain. Jesus appears in glory.

Elijah and Moses appear and talk with Jesus. Peter is so overcome he makes rather banal and inappropriate comments. A cloud overshadows them and God's voice is heard identifying Jesus as his Son. God says, 'Listen to him.'

Mark places this story here to confirm that in spite of the words about suffering, Jesus remains God's chosen one. Jesus is given divine approval. He will be shown to be God's Son, not *in spite of* his sufferings, but *because of* them.

Details of the story

We can't hear all the overtones of this story. The first Church members were still familiar with the Old Testament in a way in which we are not. But as the story was handed down, some of its detail may have become obscure to them, even to Mark. We don't know.

1   The opening words: 'Six days later' are not clear. Mark doesn't usually give exact times. Some commentators say it is a symbol. Six days was the time required for purification before you were allowed to approach God. (Exodus 24:16.)

2   Mark refers to a high mountain. People speculate which mountain. Pilgrims today visit Mount Tabor in Galilee to commemorate the story. Some place the event further north on mount Hermon, near Caesarea Philippi mentioned in 8:27. But Mark was probably not interested in geography. He was more interested in the significance of mountain tops. In the Old Testament they were the settings for meetings with God, or for supernatural revelations.

3   The term 'transfiguration' means 'to change one's form'. 'A change came over Jesus' (verse 2). The suggestion is that the three disciples had a glimpse of Jesus in his final state of glory. It is presumed that this state even extends to his clothes.

4   Elijah and Moses appear. It was a common thought at the time of Jesus that prominent Old Testament figures would reappear at the end of time. Presumably these two great figures represent the Law (Moses) and the prophets (Elijah). Their presence confirms that Jesus is the true Messiah, the fulfilment of the Law and the one to whom the prophets had looked forward. Once he has come, Moses and Elijah may retire: at the end of the story, only Jesus is to be seen (verse 8).

5   To emphasize this, the cloud appears and God speaks. In Jewish writings the cloud was the vehicle for God's real presence (called *Shekinah*). It is a regular theme in the Exodus story. To be swept up like this into the presence of God makes Peter imagine that Kingdom Come had arrived. He is again reckoning without the cross. Jesus will only be seen as the glorious Son of God in his death.

Icon of the transfiguration

Looking Deeper

Chapter 10: Journey to Jerusalem

Religious people often use the *journey* as a symbol of movement towards a goal, the truth they are looking for. The story of the Jewish people begins with Abraham's journey, just as the decisive event of Israel's history is a journey from slavery to freedom—the Exodus.

The journey, symbolic of movement towards enlightenment, knowledge or holiness, recurs again and again in all great religious traditions. It is also the theme of many works of literature, from Homer's *Odyssey* to Chaucer's *Canterbury Tales*.

Luke is the Evangelist who uses the journey theme as a literary device. But Mark hints at it too. In chapter 10 of Mark's Gospel Jesus goes on a more direct journey than any of his others. He leaves Galilee to go up to Jerusalem. It is the simple thread upon which Mark strings a number of events.

The journey in Mark

Mark indicates the movement towards Jerusalem in this way:

Mark 10:1	'Then Jesus left that place, went to the province of Judaea, and crossed the River Jordan.'
Mark 10:17	'As Jesus was starting on his way again . . .'
Mark 10:32	'Jesus and his disciples were now on the road going up to Jerusalem.'
Mark 10:46	'They came to Jericho . . .'
Mark 10:52	'At once he was able to see and followed Jesus on the road.'

Events on the journey

1   The Pharisees and divorce (10:1–12)

Some Pharisees ask Jesus for his opinion on divorce.

It was an invitation to enter a debate between two rival schools of thought. There was disagreement over interpretation of Deuteronomy 24:1. The school of Rabbi Shammai said that divorce could only be allowed for adultery and indecency. But the more liberal school of Rabbi Hillel claimed that divorce could be claimed for almost any failing of the wife, even for burning the dinner. Divorce was a simple affair whereby the man gave his wife a certificate dismissing her.

According to Mark, Jesus answers the Pharisees by lifting marriage to a higher plane. He appeals to God's original intention when creating the two sexes. He intended one male to be united to one female in a union which would not be broken. Jesus sees this as a reference to the sacredness of human relationships, and to the equal dignity of men and women. Such equality would be new to the people of his time.

The divorce permitted in the Law of Moses was only a temporary prescription for a people who were immature. Since the Kingdom, which had come with Jesus, was about restoring the original will of God for people, then an indissoluble marriage was the only suitable practice.

Pilgrim's body find

The body of a fourteenth century pilgrim unearthed in Worcester Cathedral during routine excavations to test the foundations was hailed yesterday as an important discovery.

Mr Philip Barker, the eminent archaeologist, described it as probably unique in Britain and unusual throughout Europe.

The body was wearing a leather tunic and knee length boots, and buried with it was a staff denoting a person of office. Cathedral authorities believe it may be an abbot because it was buried in the building.

Christian denominations today are not agreed on the practical application of this text. (See page 99.)

It is not clear why Mark put this debate with the Pharisees here. It may be because he felt it was an important issue and it went here as easily as anywhere else. The Roman society of Mark's contemporaries was quite permissive and divorce was easily obtained. He may be pointing out to the Christian community that discipleship was costly. It included the exacting standard demanded in the marriage relationship.

Immediately following this episode, Mark includes a scene where Jesus embraces and blesses the children. It is a popular story made famous by artists. It is probably a reflection by Mark on the early Church's practice of baptizing infants, whose trustfulness Mark sees as a perfect image of discipleship.

2   The rich young man (10:17–31)

It has been said that this is 'the most impressive piece of narrative in the whole of Mark's Gospel'. (Sean Frayne *Scripture Discussion Commentary 7* Sheed & Ward 1971.) It is a conversation between Jesus and a rich young man who asks: 'Good teacher, what must I do to receive eternal life?' It is an important question for Mark as it gives him the opportunity yet again to explain discipleship. There are some points to note.

1   As Sean Frayne remarks, Mark's skill at describing a human scene is at its best: *'Jesus looked straight at him with love...' 'When the man heard this, gloom spread over his face...'*

2   Jesus rejects the description 'good'. This doesn't mean that Jesus thought of himself as sinful, but rather that the over-enthusiasm of this man for Jesus was drawing his attention away from God himself.

3   Note that the keeping of the Commandments is presented in a very negative way. Curious. 'Do not...do not...do not.'

4   The man seems a very suitable candidate for discipleship because he has observed all the Commandments. Jesus can see that it may not have cost him very much. He asks something which is much more costly to him, namely, to give up his personal possessions.

5   The disciples' reaction is interesting. They are shocked and amazed at what Jesus demands of the young man. They don't understand that wealth can be a stumbling block to discipleship. Twice Jesus declares that wealth makes things hard, and twice the disciples are staggered by it. The disciples had always supposed, from their Jewish background, that riches and possessions were signs of God's special favour. They are being presented with the *cost* of discipleship. It is a radical demand.

6   Why should it be necessary to give up personal possessions on demand, in order to become a disciple of Jesus? Presumably because possessions give people status and security, and allow them to rely on their possessions rather than on God. Poverty is a surer way of learning the total trust required of a disciple.

7   Note that Jesus does not include 'wife' in the list in verse 29. The early Christians may have felt that the marriage union (presented as indissoluble by Mark earlier in this chapter) could not be broken even on these grounds.

'Christ blessing the children' by Nicolaes Maes (Reproduced by courtesy of the Trustees, The National Gallery, London)

8   The saying in verse 31 seems to have been a proverbial one which was in use in the early Church. It was probably unattached to any particular story, since each evangelist has found his own place for it.

9   This costly demand of discipleship leads into verse 32: 'Jesus and his disciples were now on the road up to Jerusalem...The disciples were filled with alarm.'

Summary

In this central section of the Gospel Mark develops his teaching on discipleship. It is presented in the form of a vague journey from Caesarea Philippi to Jerusalem, a journey which takes the most definite shape in chapter 10. He is accompanied by the disciples. It is in this section that Mark places all the predictions of Jesus' passion and resurrection, given privately to the disciples. Mark also includes here much teaching about the cost of discipleship. The section is introduced by a story of a blind man who receives his sight, and finishes with another blind man who receives his sight.

Here is a more visual summary of the section.

'The calling of James and John' by Marco Basaiti

Section on discipleship	
Jesus heals a blind man at Bethsaida (Mark 8:22)	
Event at Caesarea Philippi. Mark 8:27	Peter proclaims Jesus as 'Messiah-Christ'. He does not see the implications.
Call to carry the cross and follow Jesus. Mark 8:34	Jesus spells out clearly that following him means the cross. In the time of Mark that could mean, literally, death.
Transfiguration. Mark 9:2	Peter, James and John witness Jesus in glory. Peter still does not understand that suffering must come first.
Cure of the epileptic boy. Mark 9:17	The father of the boy is the true disciple longing to increase his faith. The disciples lack faith and so cannot cure the boy.
Who is the greatest? Mark 9:33	Jesus spells out discipleship in terms of humility.
An exorcist who cast out demons in Jesus' name. Mark 9:38	There was an uneasiness in the Christian community about who really belonged to the Church. This story and the sayings which follow emphasize the importance of attitudes towards other people.
Question on divorce. Mark 10:2	After the question by the Pharisees, Jesus gives his answer in private, to the disciple. Discipleship is costly.
Jesus blesses children. Mark 10:13	Discipleship is a childlike trust.
The rich man. Mark 10:17	The man cannot rise to the demands of discipleship. Wealth may not be a reward from God; it can be a stumbling block.
Jesus speaks of his death and resurrection. Request from James and John. Mark 10:32	The disciples' fear shows continued lack of understanding. So does the request for the best seats. Discipleship means service of others, and suffering.
Jesus heals blind Bartimaeus, who then 'followed Jesus on the road'. (Mark 10:52.)	

A   Short questions (Knowledge)

1   In what part of Palestine do the events described in chapters 1–7 in Mark take place?

2   What event in chapter 8 is a turning point in the Gospel?

3   Who said to Jesus, 'You are the Messiah'?

4   According to Mark, how did Jesus immediately respond to this profession of faith?

5   Which three disciples accompanied Jesus up the mountain of the Transfiguration?

6   Who was seen to appear with Jesus on the mountain?

7   What journey of Jesus is described in chapter 10 of Mark?

8   Who tried to trap Jesus over the divorce laws?

9   Why was the 'rich young man' sad?

10   Why were the ten disciples angry with James and John?

B   Longer answers (Knowledge & understanding)

1   Describe the scene at Caesarea Philippi.

2   There are three predictions of the suffering and death of Jesus in this section (one each in chapters 8, 9, 10). Write out the appropriate passages.

3   Describe in your own words the scene of the Transfiguration.

4   What are the five references to a journey in chapter 10?

C   Essays (Understanding & evaluation)

1   How are the events in chapter 8 of Mark's Gospel a turning point in his story?

2   According to Mark what happened at the scene of the Transfiguration? How do you interpret this event?

3   Describe the conversation between Jesus and the rich young man. How did the disciples react to Jesus' words?

4   Would Christians today make more impact on people if they lived in less comfort?

5   Comment on Mark's presentation of the cost of discipleship in this section. (Mark 8:22–10:52.)

D   Things to do

1   Design a series of posters on the theme of *journey and pilgrimage*.

2   Find out about journeys of great religious people, including Muhammad, Gautama and Lao-tze.

3   Working in groups or alone prepare an illustrated talk on *Christian pilgrimage*.

4   People's lives can be changed by a single event—a watershed. Compile a list of people who have experienced a 'watershed' event in their lives.

5   Write a poem called 'My journey'.

B6 Conflicts

The Way In

1   Archbishop Desmond Tutu

In 1975 Desmond Tutu was appointed Anglican Dean of Johannesburg. Since that time he has preached fearlessly in South Africa the Christian message of justice, respect and equality for all people—whatever colour their skin. Today (and now Archbishop of Capetown) he is at the centre of the struggle to dismantle the apartheid system in South Africa. He embarrasses the government by his opposition. When charged with being political he once wrote: *'If we are to say that religion cannot be concerned with politics then we are really saying that there is a substantial part of human life in which God's writ does not run. If it is not God's, then whose is it?'*

2   Victoria Gillick

Mrs Gillick is a Christian mother who is deeply concerned about the pressures on young people today. With unswerving determination she took on the task of challenging the DHSS in the courts. She was opposed to the guidelines that give doctors the right to prescribe contraceptives or to perform abortions upon girls under 16, without their parents' knowledge or consent.

3   Bruce Kent

In 1986 this Roman Catholic priest appeared in court, charged with damaging government property. For many years he has been a leading figure in the Campaign for Nuclear Disarmament. He is tireless in opposing governments, groups and individuals over the nuclear issue. His view on unilateral disarmament is not shared by all Christians; but he is personally convinced that the moral stand he advocates is the Gospel message. In 1987 he resigned from the ministry of the priest-hood, since his activity was considered too political for a priest to undertake.

4   Dr Sheila Cassidy

Doctor Cassidy will always be remembered for her courageous identification with the victims of an unjust political regime in Chile. She saw her duty as a doctor to treat the sick and injured—whatever their affiliation. For treating an enemy of the government she was imprisoned and tortured. Her experience led her to speak out more courageously than before against a corrupt system.

5　Archbishop Oscar Romero

In March 1980 Archbishop Romero was shot dead while celebrating the Eucharist in San Salvador. He had spoken out against the authorities on behalf of the poor of El Salvador. He had condemned the injustices and the violence of a regime that kept the poor in hunger and misery. He was 'the voice of those who have no voice'.

These Christians have something in common. They have all taken a firm stand on an issue that has led into conflict with authority. Archbishop Romero paid the ultimate price of such a confrontation; he paid with his life.

You may, or may not agree with the issues espoused by these five people, but it cannot be denied that they all take seriously their commitment to what they see as the 'right way'. Not many people risk the opposition this entails.

As Christians these five people are surely influenced by the attitude and behaviour of Jesus towards authority. Mark looks closely at the confrontations Jesus encountered during his ministry.

Main Issues

One striking aspect of Mark's Gospel is the frequent mention of controversy. In fact, one-sixth of the whole book is a record of controversies. Why does he present such an argumentative Jesus? Three reasons are suggested:

1　Many of the controversy stories may echo the disputes in which the early Church was engaged. Mark's readers would learn from them how to deal with criticism of Christianity.

2　One of the strongest objections to Christianity was its bold claim that Jesus was the Messiah-Christ, when everyone knew that he had died as a criminal. Mark's aim in listing the controversies is to provide proof that Jesus was no criminal. The evidence all points the other way. He was always being misunderstood. The criminals were those who opposed his teaching and healing ministry.

3　This opposition, according to Mark, was simply part of the opposition of Satan to the establishment of the Kingdom of God. Mark's Gospel is based (see page 25) on a world view which supposes that the creation of an ordered world was God's victory over the satanic forces of chaos. As time went on, these demonic forces reasserted themselves, and people looked forward to the day when God would conquer Satan once and for all. Jesus was seen as the agent of God who won this decisive victory. All opposition to him was Satan's last ditch stand. It included not only the fickle crowds who welcomed Jesus in good times, only to abandon him in bad times. It included even Jesus' followers, who again and again misunderstood him. With their stubbornness and unwillingness (see 6:52, 8:17, 16:14) they too were part of Satan's army. Peter himself was as bad as the rest, and he had to be called 'Satan' face to face (Mark 8:33). But it included above all the official authorities of Jesus' time, with their closed minds, and their fear of the changes Jesus was demanding. Jesus' wordy exchanges with them are seen by Mark as echoes of the wordy exorcism of evil spirits.

Here is a list of the fourteen 'controversy' episodes in the Gospel.

Mark 2:1–12 Controversy over healing and sin
2:13–17 Controversy over eating with outcasts
2:18–22 Controversy over fasting
2:23–3:6 Two controversies over Sabbath-breaking
3:22–30 Controversy over source of Jesus' power
7:1–23 Controversy over religious observances
8:11–12 Controversy over 'proofs'
10:2–12 Controversy over divorce
11:27–33 Controversy over Jesus' authority
12:13–17 Controversy over paying taxes
12:18–27 Controversy over rising from death
12:28–34 Controversy over most important commandment
12:35–37 Controversy over identity of Messiah

Mark seems to have placed these stories of conflict carefully into his text, since they fall roughly into two groups.

1 The first group is in chapter 2. Its stories record how the Jewish authorities, the local Pharisees and Scribes, challenge the authority of Jesus. His interpretation of the Law, and of the religious practices it demands, infuriate them. In chapter 3:22 authorities even arrive from Jerusalem to put further pressure on him. (Note that this falls *outside* the group of five.)

These first five stories contain five claims to authority which Mark wants to emphasize:

Mark 2:10 *'The Son of man has authority on earth to forgive sin.'*
2:17 *'I have not come to call respectable people, but outcasts.'*
2:19 *'Do you expect the guests at a wedding party to go without food?'*
2:28 *'The Son of man is Lord even of the Sabbath.'*
3:4 *'What does our law allow us to do on the Sabbath? To help or to harm? To save a man's life or to destroy it?'*

Mark sees Jesus as having God's power to *forgive sin*; in fact his mission is to invite *sinners* (outcasts) into the Kingdom. His presence should be the cause of *joy and celebration*. He is above the restrictions of *Law* (Sabbath), and his whole purpose is to liberate people and *bring life*. The powers that be cannot accept this. The five stories end with the ominous 'plan to kill Jesus' (3:6).

2 It is in *chapter 12* that Mark tells the Parable of the Vineyard Tenants. (See page 33.) You will remember that it represents a direct

confrontation with the authorities. When Jesus finishes telling the story the Jewish leaders try to arrest him knowing that he was getting at them (Mark 12:12). Even now they fail to see who Jesus really is.

It is around this parable that Mark sets a second series of five controversy stories. Again and again the leaders close their minds to Jesus. (Chapters 11 and 12.)

Mark's Gospel has been described as a Passion narrative with a rather long introduction. These later conflict stories are told at the beginning of the Passion narrative, when the long introduction is over. Jesus has arrived in Jerusalem to face death. Mark makes his final attempt to explain how such a thing could happen to the Son of God.

Those in authority (Pharisees, teachers of the Law, chief Priests, Sadducees) ask Jesus direct questions in order to catch him out.

Now the disciples are silent witnesses

Mark 11:28   *What right have you?*
    12:14   *Should we pay taxes?*
    12:23   *Whose wife will she be?*
    12:28   *Which is the most important commandment?*

Notice how in this section of the Gospel the disciples are only observers. The previous section had concentrated strongly on them. Now they are silent witnesses. Jesus is alone at the centre of the stage.

Looking Deeper

Here we will examine some of the controversies in more detail.

The first controversy story over the healing of the paralysed man (Mark 2:1–12), has already been dealt with on page 39. Jesus is charged with 'blasphemy', because he said to the man *'My son, your sins are forgiven.'* Only God can forgive sin. The next story of conflict follows naturally from this. It is about someone regarded as another sinner or outcast.

1   The controversy over eating with outcasts (Mark 2:13–17)

This is the story of the calling of Levi. He was a tax-collector, and in the eyes of the 'pious' Jews (Pharisees) that made him a sinner. It was a profession which was open to unjust abuses. What was worse, a tax-collector worked for the hated Roman rulers.

It was a scandal to the Pharisees that Jesus would eat at table with this outcast and his friends. It was even more of a scandal for Jesus to call Levi into his group of followers.

The whole story leads up to the saying of Jesus in verse 17. *'People who are well do not need a doctor, but only those who are sick. I have not come to call respectable people but outcasts.'* It is possible that this is the origin of the story. Mark simply finds an event which illustrates the saying, and sews the two together.

When the Evangelists are describing Jesus' action in this story, they are also defending the practice of the early Church to open wide its doors to a strange assortment of people who lived on the margins of society.

He lives on the margins of society

2 The controversy over fasting (Mark 2:18–22)

The next scene concerns fasting. The disciples of Jesus do not follow a practice of fasting at certain times, unlike the followers of the Baptist and the Pharisees. 'Some people' challenge Jesus about this.

Fasting was important to strict Jews. They looked askance at those who didn't observe this practice.

Jesus answers, typically, with a parable. As long as a bridegroom is at a wedding party the guests go on eating. They only stop when the bridegroom leaves the party. The figure of the bridegroom belongs to the Old Testament imagery of the Kingdom of God. Jesus is challenging the people to accept that the Kingdom of God is present, and he himself is the central figure in that Kingdom. His coming is a cause of celebration, not fasting.

For the early Christians there is the unmistakable lesson that 'fasting' belongs to the time of Jesus' death when the 'bridegroom' has been taken away from them. This is the way in which the Church has understood these words, and consequently encouraged fasting as an appropriate act during the time of Lent, (the season before the celebration of Easter, when Christians remember the suffering and death of Jesus.)

The further parables in verses 21–22 suggest that Mark is using this scene to comment on the radical break with the past that was demanded of the Christian community. Jesus' coming had changed everything.

3 Two controversies over Sabbath-breaking (Mark 2:23–3:6)

In these stories the conflict centres around the strict observance of the Sabbath. Some Jews had become so obsessed with the Law that their behaviour had become quite fanatical. The Law forbade work on the Sabbath (except in an emergency). Some rabbis interpreted this so strictly that people could hardly obey it. Even dragging a chair across the dirt floor of a house could be seen as 'ploughing'. When the disciples picked ears of corn as they passed by the edge of a corn field, these over-strict Jews accused them of 'harvesting' the corn.

Jesus replied as the rabbis always did, by quoting examples from the scriptures that justify him: King David had himself broken the Sabbath. (It is typical that Mark gets the quote wrong. Abiathar was not the high priest at the time, but Ahimelech.) Jesus' case is that the needs of people are more important than laws, a point made by other rabbis of his time. But in the last line of the first story (verse 28) Mark makes a stronger point. Jesus is the Son of Man. As such he is the 'Lord of the Sabbath' and therefore free of the Law.

Son of Man

The title 'Son of Man' occurs frequently in the Gospels—86 times—and hardly at all outside the Gospel pages. Since it is found exclusively on the lips of Jesus, it can safely be assumed that it was a characteristic way in which he spoke of himself.

It is difficult to know what exactly he meant by it. 'Son of Man' can have an entirely *neutral* sense, meaning no more than 'man', a member of the human race. The prophet Ezekiel used it frequently of himself, adding the idea of *weakness and suffering*, 'Poor old Ezekiel.' The book of Daniel used it as a symbol of the *humane kingdom* which would take over from a succession of bestial kingdoms (Daniel chapter 7). This symbolic 'Son of Man' was later turned into an actual individual, scarcely distinct from God himself. It was he, not the Messiah, whom many expected to come in glory from heaven to establish God's Kingdom. The title is used in *all* these senses in the Gospels. Sometimes it has *heavenly* overtones, as in Mark 13:26, '*Then the Son of Man will appear coming in the clouds with great power and glory.*' Often it has overtones of *suffering*, as in Mark 9:12, '*The Scriptures say that the Son of Man will suffer much and be rejected.*' Sometimes it is quite *neutral*, with no overtones at all, as in '*Who do people say the Son of Man is?*' (Matthew 16:13 = Mark 8:27 '*Who do people say I am?*'), or '*The Son of Man came, and he ate and drank*' (Luke 7:34).

It is possible that Jesus originally used the title in this last sense, meaning no more than 'I', as people do when they speak of themselves as 'one'. Yet because of the many overtones the words could take on, it was the ideal title to express the *one* who would bring about the *glorious* Kingdom of God through his *suffering*.

No doubt this story is a basis for the early Christian decision to observe the Lord's day on Sunday rather than Saturday.

4 The controversy over paying taxes (Mark 12:13–17)

Chapter 12 begins with the parable of the tenants in the vineyard. As we have already seen (page 33) it concludes with the Jewish leaders wanting to arrest Jesus. They are unsuccessful, so Mark represents them as setting a trap for Jesus. They waylay him, pretend to flatter him, and then cunningly set a difficult question. Is it lawful to pay taxes to the Roman Emperor?

The tax referred to was the poll-tax, imposed by Rome on all inhabitants of Palestine. It was a sore point with the Jews because it was a constant reminder of their subjection to Roman rule. A direct answer by Jesus would get him into difficulty. If he advised paying the tax, he would lose popular support. It would discredit him in the eyes of all the nationalist groups. But if he advised against paying it, he could be reported to the Roman authorities for political subversion.

Jesus avoids the difficulty. He asks them to provide the silver coin bearing the image of Caesar. He hasn't got one, and so is not compromised. They have, and so have already implicitly acknowledged Caesar's authority. This being so they are obliged to pay taxes to him.

A Roman coin

Jesus makes them spell it out for themselves by asking 'Whose face and name are these?' They reply, 'The Emperor's.' 'Well,' says Jesus 'it belongs to him then. Give it back to him!' But (he adds), 'don't forget to give back to God what has *his* face and name stamped on it—yourselves.' A neat reply. Duty to the Emperor is quite consistent with duty to God.

The whole question of subjection to a foreign power was a burning issue to the Jews at the time of Jesus. We have already seen that many thought the Messiah's role was to rid the Jews of this domination. For Mark's contemporaries too it was an issue of importance. The Christians in Nero's Rome were required to take part in emperor worship.

Jesus' reply is a reminder that all this is far less important than the demands of God's Kingdom. The coming of God's Kingdom puts all questions of earthly politics in the shade.

5 Controversy over rising from death (Mark 12:18–27)

Mark may have placed this story here, immediately after the taxes controversy, because he wanted to show that the Sadducees, as well as the Pharisees, were in opposition to Jesus.

Typically, Mark doesn't tell much about the Sadducees. This is the only time he mentions them. They were the aristocrats from whom the High Priest was chosen. (See page 14.) They didn't accept any of the new ideas introduced into Jewish beliefs by the Pharisees. They were the very right-wing conservatives. Jesus had much more in common with the Pharisees.

Behind the question in this conflict story lies a theological controversy between the two parties. It concerned the idea of resurrection after death. The Pharisees believed in a resurrection, the Sadducees didn't.

The question is posed to make Jesus look foolish. In the event Jesus' reply shows up the foolishness of the Sadducees' hypothetical question.

1 The conditions of resurrection life are so different from those of earthly life that the question is a nonsense. Resurrection is not a bringing of corpses back to life on earth.

2 The Old Testament shows that life after death is a real possibility. Abraham, Isaac and Jacob, though physically dead, were still in a *living* relationship with God. God is the God of the living. That is what resurrection is about.

6 The controversy over the most important commandment (Mark 12:28–34)

Now it is the turn of the Scribes to question Jesus. Scribes were experts in the Law. (See page 15.) There had been attempts by some rabbis to sum up, in the shortest possible form, the basic principles of the Law (while insisting that the Law should be kept in all its detail).

Perhaps this Scribe is quite simply bewildered by the sheer weight of rules and regulations. His question may not have been as hostile as the previous ones.

Mark may have placed this story here to show that Jesus was really an orthodox Jew; he was, in fact following the Law, even if the authorities thought otherwise. Here is an orthodox Jew, a strict observer of the Law, who expresses total agreement with Jesus.

The story is also an instruction for the disciples. It shows them that whilst Jesus understood the law, he was against legalism. He saw *love* as the supreme value. It has two expressions, love of God and love of neighbour. This was already understood in the Old Testament (Deuteronomy 6: 5 and Leviticus 19: 18). These two books were part of the Pentateuch or Law. All that Jesus does is to remove this commandment of love from the category of *law*, and make it instead the *attitude* that is required for disciples in the Kingdom of God. Mark has discipleship on his mind again. Here is a teacher of the Law—an unlikely person (see Mark 12: 38–40)—who is close to the Kingdom of God, because he understood what Jesus is saying.

Conclusion

For Mark, Jesus causes controversy because he forces people to a decision. He challenges people's prejudices and ideas about God. No one who listens to his word can remain neutral.

Any fixed ideas that people have, any interests that they feel the need to protect, even 'religious ones' are questioned by Jesus.

In these vivid passages, Mark is asking his readers whether they have really considered whose side they are on, the Kingdom of God that Jesus preached, or the Kingdom of Satan? Their own suffering at the hand of the world should give them an answer. If they are resentful, their very resentment is an indication that they are not on God's side.

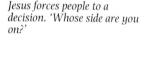

Jesus forces people to a decision. 'Whose side are you on?'

A Short answers (Knowledge)

1 How many controversy episodes are there in Mark's Gospel?

2 Name any three controversies.

3 Who was Levi?

4 Where does Mark put Jesus' saying, 'The Sabbath was made for the good of Man; man was not made for the Sabbath.'?

5 What does 'This is Corban' mean?

6 Who were the Sadducees?

7 Did the Sadducees believe in a resurrection from the dead?

8 Give another name for a teacher of the Law.

9 Who said to Jesus 'Which commandment is the most important of all'?

10 What answer did Jesus give to this question?

B Longer answers (Knowledge & understanding)

1 Name the five controversies in chapters 2–3 of Mark.

2 Name the five controversies in chapters 11–12 of Mark.

3 Tell in your own words the story of the calling of Levi.

4 Outline the controversy over paying the tax to Caesar.

5 How did the Pharisees differ from the Sadducees?

C Essays (Understanding & evaluation)

1 *The authority of Jesus is for Mark the issue behind all the conflict stories.'* Comment on this, referring to the first five controversy stories in the Gospel.

2 Outline two controversy stories, one from chapter 2 and one from chapter 12 of Mark's Gospel.

3 Describe the controversy over resurrection (Mark 12:18–27) showing how Jesus made the Sadducees look foolish by the answers he gave.

4 Why do you think Mark devotes one-sixth of his Gospel to conflict stories?

D Things to do

1 Make a collage in 14 sections to illustrate the conflict stories in this Gospel.

2 Suggest (in a visual form) 14 contemporary scenes of conflict that reflect the 14 scenes of conflict of Mark's narrative. Display them with appropriate texts from the Gospel.

3 Find out more about the people mentioned at the beginning of this chapter (The Way In).

The End is coming (Mark 13)

This is a strange and difficult section of the Gospel. It is the only time Jesus gives a long, uninterrupted speech on a single topic. It reads like the farewell speeches of great leaders of the past (Jacob, Moses). Like them, Jesus is represented as leaving a last spoken 'will and testament'.

Most commentators agree that Mark has put the speech together from various sayings of Jesus. He may himself have added a number of Jewish ideas on the same subject. This often leaves the meaning of the speech unclear.

It is made even more unclear by the strange 'apocalyptic' style in which it is expressed. *Apocalypse* means unveiling a secret. Through a number of obscure references to contemporary events, the reader is given a preview of the victory which God is secretly preparing, soon to be made clear to everyone. Many Jewish apocalypses were written in times of crisis, to give courage to persecuted people.

It is about the ending of a world and the beginning of a new age. Jesus had just foretold the final destruction of the Jerusalem Temple (it was sacked by the Roman army in the year 70). The disciples ask how they are to know when this will take place. They are told to expect trouble after trouble, especially when the Temple is desecrated by 'The Awful Horror' (verse 14, presumably a reference to a Roman statue). They are told to expect to be confused by false claims. But there will be no doubts left when the Son of Man (see page 60) finally comes to vindicate those who have persevered. The new age will have dawned.

Points to notice

1   The discourse would be of great interest to the early Church, which lived in high hopes of a glorious 'Second Coming' of Christ. It was thought this would happen soon.
2   The discourse is spoken only to Jesus' closest companions—Peter, James, John and Andrew. Even at this stage, Mark continues to be keen on his theme of 'secrecy' (see page 87).
3   Mark also stresses another favourite theme—the difficulty of being a genuine disciple of Jesus. The chapter is meant to console and encourage. But it is also full of warnings. To be Son of God cost Jesus dearly. His followers cannot expect to get by on the cheap.

    Jesus accepted suffering, ridicule and rejection. In this he was setting the example for his disciples. His sufferings were not a substitute for their own. Those who think they can follow Jesus and escape the cross have mistaken who the true Messiah is (verse 21).
4   Yet the overall feel of the chapter is optimistic. The chapters which follow will tell of Jesus' final suffering. He dies. But that death must not obscure the victory and glory promised in chapter 13.
5   It is probable that the chapters which follow were already written before Mark took them over. Chapter 13 is therefore Mark's own conclusion to the part of the Gospel he personally composed. It has an urgency about it which is very typical of Mark.

B7 The suffering and death of Jesus

The Way In

You won't have very far to look for a cross. If you are a Christian you might have one hanging on the wall at home. You'll certainly have a book with a cross in it. You may have one round your neck. Have a look round the churches in your area and see how they display the cross.

Over the ages, millions of Christians have gone on pilgrimage to Jerusalem. Most of them have brought back an emblem of the cross. Pilgrims still do this today. Here is the Jerusalem cross, as worn by today's pilgrims. Unless, of course, they have discovered a little antique, one of thousands dug up in the Holy City.

Why is the cross such an important emblem for Christian people? It is because they see in it the clearest expression of what Christianity is about.

Throughout the ages artists have capitalized on this. They have represented the cross in marble, in ivory, in wood, in gold, in oils, in jewels. Sometimes the cross is empty, sometimes it carries the body of Jesus. Each age has emphasized different aspects of what the cross means to Christians.

Look at the following examples.

1   The Church emerged triumphant after its early confrontation with Rome. As a result the earliest representations of the cross are like this one, sculpted on a sarcophagus (AD 340). It is a victorious cross—with a laurel wreath. This is not really how Mark saw the cross of Jesus.

2   This painting is from the Basilica of Sts Cosmas and Damian in Rome. It is a Byzantine crucifixion figure of the 8th century. Jesus is clothed in the rich robes of the Byzantine King, crowned and alive. The anguish of the cross is missing. This is not really how Mark saw Jesus.

3   By the 12th century the figure on the cross was more austere. But, as this example from a German liturgical book shows, the figure is delicate and serene. Too serene for Mark. That is not really how he saw Jesus crucified.

4   The Grünewald painting (around 1500) is a better reflection of Mark's understanding of the death of Jesus. He died an agonizing death as a criminal. There were blood, tears, anguish and pain.

1

2

3

4

5 *Life is a cross to bear for this little Arab refugee*

5   Mark wrote his Gospel to explain to suffering Christians that no one can be a son of God without getting into deep trouble. Jesus first and then his followers. That is why the picture alongside could also be, for Mark, a representation of crucifixion.

The Main Issues

Christians celebrate Jesus' last days during a short period before Easter, called 'Holy Week'. It begins with a commemoration of Jesus' entry into Jerusalem (Palm Sunday). How does Mark tell this story?

Jesus enters Jerusalem (Mark 11:1–10)

Jesus approaches Jerusalem in a solemn procession. Mark's account is rich in Old Testament references. He describes how Jesus rode into the City on a donkey. It was a dramatic action. The prophets in the Old Testament made similar gestures when their words went unheeded. (See 1 Kings 11:29ff, Jeremiah 27:1–11, Ezekiel 4:1–3.) The ride into the city was a simple gesture, not the triumphant procession of a warrior. Many of Jesus' followers expected him to defeat the Romans and finally be proclaimed as Messiah. The ride was to prove them wrong.

But what really happened? We don't know.

1   Jesus could have ridden into Jerusalem almost unnoticed; other pilgrims were doing the same. They were all welcomed with the waving palms and the words of blessing. Perhaps it was only *in retrospect* that Mark linked the event with an Old Testament text.

2   The text in Mark's mind is Zechariah's:

Rejoice, rejoice, people of Zion!
Shout for joy, you people of Jerusalem!
Look, your king is coming to you!
He comes triumphant and victorious,
but humble and riding on a donkey,
on a colt, the foal of a donkey.
                                    Zechariah 9:9

Palm procession in Jerusalem today

If the story of Jesus' ride into Jerusalem records an actual *historical* event, then it would have had to be carefully planned. Jesus would have been setting out deliberately to fulfil the Zechariah text. He would have been openly claiming to be the Messiah.

Which of the two explanations is more likely?

This entry into Jerusalem is also described in the other three Gospels. It is interesting to notice how the other Evangelists alter the text. Luke introduces the word 'peace'. Mark doesn't use the word, but even so, the event itself is above all about peace. Jesus, by his action, was coming into Jerusalem as a lover of peace, not as a conquering hero. Kings rode into battle on horses, but on donkeys when they came in peace. If the disciples wanted a national leader to free them from the Romans, they would have to look for someone else. So the long journey is over and the destination is reached. Jesus is in Jerusalem to undergo his passion and to die. In Luke's Gospel that is it. The city is reached once and for all. But Mark has Jesus coming and going between Jerusalem and Bethany.

Mark 11:11   *'Jesus entered Jerusalem, and went into the Temple . . . But since it was already late in the day, he went out to Bethany.'*

    11:15   *'When they arrived in Jerusalem . . .'*

    11:27   *'They arrived once again in Jerusalem.'*

    14:3   *'Jesus was in Bethany . . .'*

However, Mark is anxious for us to know that the time of suffering is approaching. In verse 18 of chapter 11 we are told that: 'The chief priests and the teachers of the Law . . . began looking for some way to kill Jesus. There follows a series of confrontations which provide the background for the final betrayal. (See pages 56 to 62.)

Jesus is anointed at Bethany (Mark 14: 3–9)

The story of the woman who anointed Jesus with expensive perfume is probably one of the many stories about Jesus in circulation long before Mark wrote the Gospel. It is a good example of a story used by the four evangelists, but with many variations. John puts it into his text *before* the entry into Jerusalem. Luke places it at a completely different time in Jesus' life (Luke 7: 36) because he can't have Jesus in Bethany after he had reached Jerusalem. (See above.)

The story shows the devotion that ordinary people were showing towards Jesus, and illustrates his compassion and concern for people who were considered outcasts. One interesting detail is that whereas Luke and John describe an anointing of Jesus' feet, Mark—followed by Matthew—speaks of the woman anointing the *head* of Jesus. It would seem that Mark is thinking of the anointing of the head that is associated with the idea of the Messiah. (The word means 'the anointed one'.) He deliberately places this story as a prelude to the Passion and Death of Jesus. His readers should understand that it was the Messiah himself who was hunted down by the authorities (verses 1 and 2) and then betrayed by Judas, one of the twelve disciples (verses 10 and 11).

> The stories that now follow (The Last Supper, the Agony in Gethsemane and the Way of the Cross) are three presentations of the Passion of Jesus. The actual outward drama of Jesus' suffering was by way of the cross. The two stories that precede it prepare the way, and give an inner meaning to the Passion.

Jesus' Last Supper (Mark 14:12–31)

The memory of Jesus' last days has always been of central importance to Christians. Above all, they cannot forget the last words he spoke with them, and the last meal he ate with them.

It was natural for the early Church to re-enact this last supper of Jesus and to make of it the characteristic worship of the Church. It is still celebrated under different names: the Liturgy, the Mass, the Communion Service, the Eucharist and the Lord's Supper.

The meal and the Passover

Mark, Matthew and Luke place the Last Supper in the setting of the Jewish Passover meal. (Read Mark 14:12–16.) The Passover was the greatest of Jewish feasts. It was celebrated at full moon in the month of Nisan (March–April). It commemorated the escape of their ancestors from Egyptian slavery. (Read Exodus 12:26–17:16.) Pilgrims flocked to Jerusalem for a festival which lasted a whole week—Feast of Unleavened Bread—and which began with the Passover meal.

Soldiers mingle with pilgrims in Jerusalem today

Because of the great crowds attracted by this feast, and the emotions it aroused, there was usually trouble in the city. This restless scene is the backdrop to the last days of Jesus' life. The authorities, intent on arresting Jesus but afraid of causing riots themselves, were grateful for Judas' unexpected help.

Mark's story

Mark describes how a disillusioned disciple of Jesus, Judas Iscariot, betrayed him. (Mark 14:10–11.) Mark offers no explanation for Judas' behaviour. John later put it down to greed. Some think that Judas was a Zealot who finally lost patience with Jesus over his non-violent policy. Whatever the reason, Mark adds a note (14:18–20) that Judas didn't take Jesus by complete surprise. He had already predicted the betrayal and he freely accepted it. It was in accordance with the will of God as recorded in the Old Testament.

Mark describes the preparation for the Passover meal in 14:12–16. The description is very similar to the preparation for Palm Sunday in 11:1–7. Mark is not all that interested in the correct details of the festival. He writes as if everything happened on the same day, although in reality the lambs had to be slaughtered the previous day.

Nor does Mark say very much about the meal itself (14:22–26). The early Christians really had little interest in its details, only in its religious significance. The Church in fact selected two aspects to emphasize:
1 The liturgical meal which foretold the meaning of Jesus' death.
2 The farewell meal at which Jesus gave his last commands to his followers.

1 The liturgical meal (Eucharist)

Mark and his readers interpreted this last meal of Jesus as a sacred ritual. Paul had already interpreted it in the same way many years earlier (see 1 Corinthians 11:24–25).

Why is this meal so important?

2 The farewell meal

Mark makes very little of this aspect. Luke and John will later emphasize the final discourse of Jesus to his disciples, whereas in Mark he hardly speaks a word. It is obvious that the Evangelists felt quite free to adapt their material.

Jesus in agony (Read Mark 14:32–41)

Mark jumps quite suddenly from the scene of the supper to the place called Gethsemane (oil-press), at the foot of the Mount of Olives. Jesus goes there to pray. He is in great distress. His anguish is in stark contrast with the unsuspecting sleep of the three disciples. The friends of Jesus don't come out very well in the story. Some commentators suggest that Peter probably told the story against himself. He is called Simon again by Jesus, his old name. He wasn't acting like a 'Petra', a rock of strength at this time. However, the historical accuracy of the story is questioned by many commentators. They ask how anyone *could* know how Jesus prayed, and what words he used. The prayer, they say, is a model for Christians in similar distress.

It is in the spirit of the Old Testament Psalms. They point out that Jesus prays three times and three times the disciples sleep. They suggest it corresponds to the threefold denial of Peter which Jesus has so recently predicted and which will soon come to pass.

Jesus is arrested and crucified

Here we will simply outline the series of events as Mark records them.

Jesus is arrested (Mark 14:43–52)

Jesus is still speaking to his disciples when a crowd arrives, led by Judas Iscariot. He greets Jesus as any disciple would greet his rabbi, with a kiss. He has already told the authorities that he will identify Jesus for them (in the dark?) in this way. The disciples make a faint attempt to defend Jesus by drawing swords. A sword injures the High Priest's slave, cutting off his ear. The disciples panic and run away.

Mark concludes with a strange scene of a young man, scantily dressed who runs away—leaving his clothes in the hands of a soldier. It has been suggested that this man was Mark himself. Just as Alfred Hitchcock wrote himself a very brief walk-on part in each of his films, so Mark places himself—for a moment—in his own text. It would make him a genuine eye-witness of events.

Jesus before the Council (Mark 14:53–65)

Jesus is taken to the High Priest (Caiaphas, but not named by Mark). Mark says that the trial starts straight away.

The elders, chief priests and teachers meet together. They are looking for evidence to convict Jesus, but they cannot come to any agreement because the evidence is conflicting. They ask Jesus the crucial question: '*Are you the Messiah?*' For the first time in Mark's Gospel, Jesus is absolutely straight about his identity. '*I am.*' In a sense, the Messianic Secret is out. Mark needs to present Jesus' contemporaries formally and deliberately rejecting Jesus.

Yet in another sense the true climax is still to come. Jesus is more than the political Messiah of popular expectations. He claims to be Son of (the Blessed) God (verse 61), seated on the right of the Almighty (verse 62). To his listeners, this is blasphemy, deserving the death sentence.

Jerusalem

Peter denies Jesus (Mark 14: 66–72)

Meanwhile Peter is hovering in the courtyard of the house. As he warms himself at the fire a servant and bystanders recognize him as a companion of Jesus. Frightened at what is happening he denies he ever knew Jesus. On the third denial he remembers what Jesus had said, and bursts into tears.

Jesus before Pilate (Mark 15: 1–15)

Early in the morning the priests, elders and teachers 'and the whole Council' make their plans. The Council was known as the Sanhedrin, and consisted of seventy-one members under the presidency of the High Priest. It was the highest judicial authority in the land. They had charged Jesus with blasphemy but it was only Rome that could impose the death penalty, and Rome needed a political rather than a religious motive. So Jesus is led in chains to Pilate, the Roman Governor.

Pilate asks him 'Are you the King of the Jews?' Presumably that is now the accusation. Rome would disapprove of anyone claiming kingship. Jesus avoids a direct answer, then remains silent. Pilate is amazed at Jesus, and suspects that he is innocent. He attempts to free him by reminding the crowd that a prisoner is set free at Passover. The inflamed crowd want Barabbas set free—an ironic situation since Barabbas' crime was treason against Rome. Pilate is weak, afraid of the crowd, so he gives in and sentence is passed. Mark puts the blame squarely on the shoulders of the Jews, although the Romans were implicated.

The soldiers mock Jesus (Mark 15: 16–20)

The whole company of soldiers mock Jesus and show their contempt by putting a king's robe on him. They put a crown of thorny twigs on his head. In the excavations of the Antonia fortress a Roman pavement is shown which was probably the fortress's courtyard. Letters and figures are scratched into some of the stones which suggest there was a corner used by the guards to play the game of 'King', a kind of snakes and ladders game which made fun of a mock king. The soldiers lead Jesus away to be crucified.

A soldiers' game scratched on the pavement

'Christ mocked' by Bosch

The way of the cross

Jesus is crucified (Mark 15:21–31)

Mark is very brief about the journey to the place of execution, Skull Hill or Golgotha. He simply tells how Simon, a North African, is ordered to help Jesus carry the cross. The soldiers try to give him some wine mixed with myrrh—perhaps to alleviate the agony of crucifixion. Mark says Jesus refused the drug in order to remain clear-headed to the end.

Then Jesus is crucified and the soldiers gamble for his clothes. The accusation 'The King of the Jews' is posted up on the cross. Two criminals are crucified alongside him; they and bystanders insult and taunt Jesus.

Mark's account of the last few hours of Jesus' life is remarkably impersonal in its tone. It is presumably not an eye-witness account. It seems to have three aims:

1   The Simon of Cyrene incident is meant to prove a trustworthy source of information.
2   The attitude of the priests, teachers and bystanders again emphasizes the hostility of the Jewish authorities and their supporters.
3   The whole account establishes that everything is in fulfilment of the Old Testament predictions, and is therefore according to God's will.
    (a) They gave him a drink (verse 23)
    (b) They threw dice for his clothes (verse 24)
    (c) He shared the fate of criminals (verse 28)
    (d) Bystanders mocked him (verse 29–32)
    See Psalms 22 and 69 and Isaiah 53.

Jesus dies (Mark 15:33–41)

Mark says that darkness covered the earth for three hours before Jesus died. At three o'clock he cried out '*My God, my God, why did you abandon me?*' These are words taken from Psalm 22. Commentators point out that although they sound like words of despair the psalm is, in fact, one of trust and confidence in God. For the early Christians Jesus *was* the suffering figure depicted in this psalm.

Jesus died. Mark says the curtain of the Temple was torn in two. Anyone who has ever tried to tear a hanging curtain from top to bottom will realize that this detail is symbolic. The Temple curtain separated God's 'dwelling-place' from ordinary people. To say that it was torn down means that the barrier between God and the world has been removed. That, says Mark, is the dramatic meaning of Jesus' death.

In the next verse, Mark represents the army officer in charge of the execution squad making his profession of faith '*This man was really the Son of God.*' It is the climax of the Gospel. 'Son of God' is the title Mark gave Jesus in the opening line of his book. It has been confirmed again and again by voices from heaven and from hell. But no human voice has acknowledged Jesus as 'Son of God' until this moment. It is only when one has seen Jesus die, killed by his opponents, that one knows what being 'Son of God' means. Only now does the title make sense. This verse sums up Mark's Gospel.

It is interesting that Luke puts different words in the man's mouth: '*Certainly he was a good man.*' And that sums up Luke's Gospel.

Mark adds the comment that some women were watching all this from a distance. They are probably included to prepare the way for their presence in the burial scene and what was to follow.

The burial of Jesus

The burial story was important for the early Christians. It established that Jesus had *really* died. The women who 'saw where the body of Jesus was placed' (15:47) were among those who discovered the empty tomb.

According to Old Testament law (Deuteronomy 21:22) a body could not be left hanging overnight after an execution. Joseph of Arimathea bravely asks for the body of Jesus and prepares it for burial. He places him in a tomb carved from a rock and rolls a stone against the door. Joseph does not appear anywhere else in Mark's Gospel. He is said to be a high official and a man who waited for the coming of the Messiah. It isn't clear whether he recognized that the Kingdom of God had come with Jesus, or whether he was simply a good pious Jew who buried Jesus in order to prevent the law being broken.

'The deposition' by Giotto

Looking Deeper

What is the meaning of Jesus' death?

From the earliest times, Christians have claimed that the most important moment in the drama of Jesus was his death. What a paradox! Why should dying be the most worthwhile thing Jesus ever did? Why call *that* good news?

From St Paul onwards, Christian thinkers have wrestled with this question. They have used various metaphors to try to open out this insight—the metaphors of a judge in a law-court needing to deal out justice, of a legal contract needing to be kept, of an angry person needing to be calmed down, of slaves needing to be bought back, of God's rights needing to be acknowledged by the slaughter of lambs, etc.

These metaphors have helped people in the past to make some sense of Jesus' death. But they don't speak very clearly to people today. Nor does Mark seem to think along these lines. For him Jesus' death is simply the inevitable fate of a spokesman for God in a wicked world. The whole Old Testament had constantly said the same.

People easily give lip-service to God. They claim to love, honour and obey him. But when his spokesman appears, and makes demands which threaten their way of life, they kill him. To be crucified therefore, says Mark, is not an indication that someone is not the Son of God: it could be the ultimate proof that he is! Jesus *had* to suffer (see Mark 8:31, 9:12, 14:21, 14:49). Jesus is the promised Messiah not *in spite of* the cross, but *because of* it.

Mark sees the cross therefore as the crucial test of faithfulness to God. Jesus was totally faithful, and so died. Utter failure? The very opposite. This death reveals clearly, perhaps for the first time, the extent to which human values have to give way for God's Kingdom (Rule) to be established on earth. The veil is torn away. The true God appears, no longer hidden behind comfortable compromises. Now, even pagans (the Roman centurion) can see what being the son of God is about.

> **"I don't think we Christians have understood what carrying the cross means. We are not carrying the cross when we are poor or sick or suffering small everyday things — these are all part of life. The cross comes when we try to change things. That is how it came for Jesus."**
>
> Fr Miguel D'Escoto,
> Nicaraguan Foreign Minister

Mark, therefore hails Jesus' martyr-death as a victory, not a defeat.

A new human race has been born, consisting of men and women as faithful to God as Jesus was. For Jesus did not die *in their place*, to save them the bother of dying. They too are called to be 'martyrs'—that is, to 'bear witness' to the point of death, to show that they share Jesus' understanding of God. This is the only way in which God's Kingdom can come about. It is a costly way.

Mark's is a demanding Gospel.

A Quick answers (Knowledge)

1 How did Jesus enter Jerusalem on 'Palm Sunday'?

2 What event was celebrated at the Passover Feast?

3 Where did Jesus and his disciples eat the Passover meal?

4 Who said, 'I will never leave you, even though all the rest do.'?

5 What was the Sanhedrin?

6 Why was Barabbas in prison?

7 What name was given to the place of execution?

8 Who was Simon of Cyrene?

9 What 'notice of accusation' was fixed to the cross?

10 What words did Mark say Jesus cried out from the cross?

B Longer answers (Knowledge & understanding)

1 Outline the parts played by (i) Judas Iscariot and (ii) Pilate, during the last days of Jesus.

2 List the events of Holy Week (in sequence), as Mark presents them.

3 Describe the preparation for the Passover meal and briefly outline what happened at the meal itself.

4 Write a paragraph about Peter's denial of Jesus.

5 Describe the burial of Jesus.

C Essays (Understanding & evaluation)

1 Give an account of the woman anointing Jesus with expensive perfume, as told by Mark. Why do you think Mark placed the story at this point in his Gospel?

2 Describe the scene in Gethsemane before Jesus is arrested. Do you think this is historically accurate? Comment on other possibilities.

3 Describe the Last Supper scene. What was the religious significance of this meal for the early Church? And for the churches today?

4 There are variations in the way Mark and Luke present the Passion narrative. Look for some of the differences and try to account for them.

5 Look again at the poster illustration on page 2. How does Jesus save sinners?

D Things to do

1 Collect as many pictures of the cross as you can. Display them and hold a class/group discussion about them.

2 Make a frieze of the Passion story. Use only contemporary pictures to illustrate suffering, rejection and death.

3 Read page 72 again. Find a copy of the 11th century hymn: '*Bring, all ye dear-brought nations, bring*' and notice which images are used by the writer.

4 Prepare a public reading of Mark's Passion. Make use of music, slides or pictures.

5 Compose a Passion song or a suffering poem.

B8 The Resurrection

The Way In

1

This is the same mother and child before and after life-saving medical care

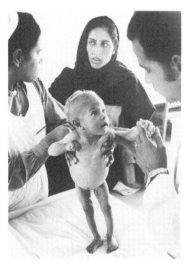 

2   From 'Kilvert's Diary'

Monday 24 May 1875
This afternoon I walked over to Lanhill. As I came down from the hill into the valley across the golden meadows and among the flower-scented hedges a great wave of emotion and happiness stirred and rose up within me. I know not why I was so happy, nor what I was expecting, but I was in a delirium of joy; it was one of the supreme few moments of existence, a deep delicious draught from the strong sweet cup of life. It came unsought, unbidden, at the meadow stile, it was one of the flowers of happiness scattered for us and found unexpectedly by the wayside of life. It came silently, suddenly, and it went as it came, but it left a long lingering glow and glory behind as it faded slowly like a gorgeous sunset, and I shall ever remember the place and the time in which such great happiness fell upon me.
                  Kilvert's Diary Ed William Plomer Jonathan Cape Ltd

3   Jim

Jim is severely brain-damaged. His mental handicap is so severe that he has lived in hospital all his young life. In all these years he has never expressed any emotion in his face; he cannot talk; he cannot hear. He can hardly see.

    A group of young people visited the hospital and offered to share their enjoyment of movement and music with the handicapped. Eventually a film was made (*Give us The Chance* Landscape Films 1983) to show how physical activities can help the mentally handicapped, and bring great enjoyment to them. One sequence was shot at Jim's hospital. The visiting students had created a simple apparatus to help the most disabled to rock and move with a soothing rhythm. The camera caught, in a fleeting moment, the face of Jim. He was swinging gently to and fro. For the first time, a glimmer of life appeared on his face.

4   Report from Southern Lebanon

The Times. June 25 1985

way e, a

More bitter fruits were sown in Southern Lebanon. We are sitting in a home in Tyre, under Israeli occupation. The family are Shia Muslims. The old hadji rests on the sofa, watching the Arabic service of Israeli television, her black gown down to her ankles, her white scarf tied round her face. Her son Ibrahim – big, tall, impetuous sits beside her. On the television is a film of the funeral of Israeli soldiers killed by a Shia Muslim suicide car bomber.

On the screen, an Israeli mother is holding her hands to her face, wailing in grief, and a rabbi is saying a prayer for the dead. The woman's cries come out clearly on the sound-track. And suddenly Ibrahim notices that his mother, the old hadji, is herself weeping.

"Why do you cry for Jews?" he asks impatiently. He calls them "Jews", not "Israelis". Then, very quietly and with great dignity, the old lady turns to him, "They have mothers, too", she says.

rut

Robert Fisk

5   A bag of bones

A father tells of the child he adopted.

I shall never forget the first time I held him in my arms, with those enormous black eyes staring at me out of his sad little face. Though he was 7 months old, he weighed only 8 lbs, little more than a newborn babe. A month before, when they had found him, half abandoned, he was a bag of bones weighing only 4 lbs, and smelling of death. One of the nuns who rescued him decided there was only one hope—to hold him close to her for 48 hours. Her body-warmth brought him to life. We worried, of course, about the long term physical, mental and psychological damage which such an unpromising start might cause. Six years later the answer is obvious. He's a bundle of energy, intelligent wit and goodness. But then they had always told me that the resurrection-body is more glorious than the one that died.

Resurrection means life triumphing over death. There is a resurrection in each of these stories—the victory of goodness and love over evil, hate and fear. In what way is the story of Jesus' resurrection different?

Jesus died as a criminal. His disciples were shattered and close to despair. All their hopes for the future were dashed. Then something happened to dispel their darkness. This is how Mark describes it.

Very early on Sunday morning, at sunrise, they went to the tomb. On the way they said to one another, 'Who will roll away the stone for us from the entrance to the tomb?' (It was a very large stone.) Then they looked up and saw that the stone had already been rolled back. So they entered the tomb, where they saw a young man sitting on the right, wearing a white robe—and they were alarmed. 'Don't be alarmed,' he said. 'I know you are looking for Jesus of Nazareth, who was crucified. He is not here—he has been raised!'

Mark 16: 2–6

The Main Issues

We'll never know exactly what happened at the weekend following Jesus' death. It wasn't videoed! Clearly something extraordinary did occur, because it changed the entire course of events. But what exactly this was, the four Gospels have expressed in quite different stories. For example Mark does not bother to relate any appearances of the risen Jesus, Matthew tells of appearances in Galilee, Luke confines all the appearances to Jerusalem.

The resurrection stories begin with an empty tomb. But first read the whole of chapter 16 of Mark and notice the different endings of the Gospel.

The women visit the tomb (Mark 16:1–8)

The burial of Jesus had been hurried and the women had no time to embalm the body. Mary Magdalene and Mary, mother of Joseph, had watched at a distance. So early on Sunday morning, Mary Magdalene and two friends, Salome and Mary, mother of James (possibly also the mother of Joseph) go to the tomb with spices, in order to anoint the body of Jesus. The tomb is empty. A young man in white tells them not to be afraid. '*He is not here,*' he says, '*he has been raised.*' The young man instructs them to tell the disciples, especially Peter, that Jesus will meet them in Galilee. The three women are terrified and run away without saying anything to anyone.

Mark's story is dramatic, with the women awestruck, speechless with fear. Now read the other Gospel accounts of the story and note differences. (Matthew 28:1–10, Luke 24:1–12, John 20:1–10.) Luke, for example, has a more gentle account of the empty tomb story. In his version there is a different group of women. They are frightened at first but gradually begin to understand the message given to them by *two* men. They go and tell the Apostles—who are the ones to disbelieve the story.

Mark's Gospel ends abruptly at verse 8 (according to the most reliable ancient manuscripts). He ends almost in the middle of a sentence; he seems to abandon the reader in the middle of the story. As Morna Hooker puts it: '*We feel let down, left in mid-air, hovering on the edge of Easter, with nothing in the way of evidence except a few women's tale of an empty tomb. We expected more than this.*' (Morna Hooker *The Message of Mark* Epworth Press 1983.

Two very early editors felt the same and attempted to complete the story.

1 Verses 9–20. These accounts of three appearances of Jesus (Mary Magdalene, two disciples, the eleven), and then of his ascension into heaven, are written in a different style. Most commentators accept that they were added later, by someone who took pieces from the Gospels of Matthew, Luke and John.

2 Some manuscripts have an even shorter ending to the Gospel: '*The women went to Peter and his friends and gave them a brief account of all they had been told. After this, Jesus himself sent out through his disciples from the east to the west the sacred and ever-living message of eternal salvation.*' This also is not in Mark's style.

The other three Evangelists completed their Gospels with several stories of the risen Christ. Why did Mark stop so abruptly? There are some possible explanations.

1 It has been supposed by some that Mark's book didn't in fact end there. The end of his Gospel has been lost.
2 Some say that Mark may have been arrested or died before he could complete the work.
3 A more recent suggestion is that Mark concluded his writing at verse 8 quite deliberately. He ends on a note of fear.

People who have studied all four Gospels closely have noticed that each Evangelist ends his Gospel in a way that exactly suits the spirit of the entire work.

Read Mark 16:8. Mark ends with a description of human failure. On close reflection, this ending is completely in character with the whole Gospel.

Throughout Mark's story the human reaction to Jesus has been fear, amazement and disbelief. The women at the tomb are reacting as most of the characters in the story have always acted.

If this *is* Mark's ending to his Gospel, then he is not offering his readers conclusive evidence. All we have is the witness of the women. (And ancient law required two *men* to witness in order to establish the truth.) They have watched the death of Jesus, noted the place of burial, and discovered the empty tomb. Now they are terrified and dumb-struck. They had been asked by the messenger to 'Go and tell his disciples'. They obey the first part of the command and rush out of the tomb. But then, confronted by the awesome truth they, like all the others, fail. They lack the courage to get going and proclaim what they know.

Mark surely wants the reader to take note of the messenger's words: '*He is going to Galilee ahead of you.*' It picks up a passage in chapter 14:28, where Jesus tells his followers, at the last meal, '*After I am raised to life, I will go to Galilee ahead of you.*' Jesus, says Mark, constantly goes on ahead, and his followers fail to keep up with him. But even after the disciples' miserable performance during the Passion and Death of Jesus, Jesus still acknowledges them as his followers and invites them all over again. There is hope, therefore, for everyone.

Mark is inviting his readers, weak human beings who constantly fail too, who are slow to *see* what is true about Jesus and who are afraid of the consequences, to start again to become disciples, followers of Jesus, the Son of God. Remember that Mark was writing during the Roman persecutions. It needed much courage to be a disciple then.

The women are terrified and dumb-struck

Looking Deeper

Ten years before Mark published his Gospel, the apostle Paul was writing to the Christians in Corinth:

> *If Christ has not been raised from the dead then we have nothing to preach and you have nothing to believe.*
>
> 1 Corinthians 15:14

This bold statement indicates how central the resurrection has always been to the Christian message. No resurrection, no Christianity. All the same, the question can still be asked: What *sort* of reality is this resurrection? What could the people who witnessed it actually have seen and heard, felt and touched?

1   Is there an answer in the Gospels?

Not really, given the kind of writings the Gospels are. They cannot be read as straight histories or biographies, as if they give a blow by blow account of what actually happened. The Evangelists did not have the materials for that. All they had was a collection of sayings and stories which expressed what Jesus meant for his first followers. And they used these stories in a very free manner, imposing their own order on them, and adding the kind of detail that best suited their purpose.

The resurrection stories follow this pattern. The Evangelists have all chosen different stories to tell what the resurrection means for them—

a guarded or unguarded tomb,
one angel or two,
one public appearance of Jesus or many,
appearances only in Jerusalem or only in Galilee,
ascension on day three or on day forty.

In the past, assuming that these stories were all historical, people have simply strung them together into a single sequence. Today scholars are more critical. Most of them assure us this cannot be done without cheating. They ask whether the Evangelists ever meant the stories to be taken as factual descriptions of observable events. Could the stories have some other purpose?

2   The empty tomb

The story of an empty tomb is to be found in all four Gospels. It cannot be dismissed, therefore, as a later invention. It is part of a very early Easter tradition.

All the same, it does not seem to be an *essential* part of the Easter story, since Paul (writing even earlier than the Gospels) is happy to speak of the resurrection simply in terms of Jesus appearing to his friends. He makes no mention of the empty tomb.

> *I passed on to you what I have received, which is of the greatest importance: that Christ died for our sins, as written in the Scriptures; that he was buried and that he was raised to life three days later, as written in the Scriptures; that he appeared to Peter and then to all twelve apostles. Then he appeared to more than five hundred of his followers at once, most of whom are still alive, although some have died. Then he appeared to James, and afterwards to all the apostles. Last of all he appeared also to me . . .*

1 Corinthians 15: 3–8

Icon of St Paul

Paul does not find it necessary to refer to an empty tomb. Does he simply assume that it *was* empty? Or is the empty tomb not a photographable reality at all—simply a *dramatic way* of saying that although Jesus died, he is not among the dead? He is now to be found not in a graveyard, but in the midst of the Christian community. It is this community which now forms the risen 'body' of Christ, which now 'embodies' the risen Jesus. (Is this the kind of reality that the empty tomb stories are actually about?)

3   The Appearances

Matthew, Luke and John all have stories of Jesus appearing to his friends after his death. Mark does not, though he promises that Jesus will appear after the Gospel ends. The appendix (16:9–20) adds a paraphrase of appearance stories borrowed from the other three Evangelists.

What kind of reality stands behind these appearance stories? Something that could have been videoed? Paul does not seem to think so. He says that the risen Christ appeared to him too, years later, when he was converted on the Damascus road. But it was a vision none of his companions could see (Acts 9:7). Yet he uses exactly the same word of this appearance as he does of the earlier appearances of Jesus to the disciples. (See the text of 1 Corinthians above.)

Could it be that the stories of 'seeing' Jesus refer to an inward vision rather than an outward one, an *insight* into Jesus rather than a physical *sight* of him? If this were so, then the vivid details of the risen Jesus speaking and eating and being touched would again be *a dramatic way* of emphasizing that the presence of Jesus was experienced as a reality, not as mere wishful thinking. In the Christian community Jesus truly lived on, as anyone who entered that community could witness.

4   Conclusion

What really happened after Jesus died?

Non-believers say nothing happened. People simply began to imagine things. Believers deny that nothing happened. Something had to take place to convince the friends of Jesus that he lives on beyond death.

Some would express this 'something' in physical terms. To say that Jesus lives on beyond death can only be true if the Easter stories are taken literally. The stone was literally rolled away. The tomb was literally empty, and the angels guarding it literally spoke to the disciples. Jesus literally appeared to his friends and spoke to them in a way which could have been filmed and taped.

There are Christians who do not treat the Easter stories so literally. This does not mean they want to discard the stories. On the contrary, they recognize them as expressing most powerfully and successfully the meaning of Easter, but in the way that poetry and drama can express reality more deeply than mere statements of fact. They interpret the stories as vivid ways of conveying what all Christians believe: that Jesus' death was not the end of his story, but only the beginning. Their experience is that Jesus lives on in their lives, and that is the 'something' that really happened. They, therefore, believe the resurrection not because someone had told them about it, but because they too claim to 'see' the risen Jesus even today. For them believing is seeing.

The risen Jesus (drawing of a cross in the convent, Saint-Brieuc, France)

A   Short answers (Knowledge)
1   According to Mark who visited the tomb on Sunday morning?
2   Who was found sitting in the tomb?
3   What message was given to be passed on to the disciples?
4   What was the reaction of these women?
5   Are the four Gospel accounts of the resurrection remarkable for their similarity or their dissimilarity?
6   Mark's Gospel seems to end abruptly. A later editor attempted to tidy it up by mentioning three further appearances of Jesus. What were they?
7   According to Mark's Gospel where were the appearances of Jesus to take place?
8   Is the story of an empty tomb found in all four Gospels?
9   What happened to Jesus after the appearances?
10   What happened to the disciples after this?

B   Longer answers (Knowledge & understanding)
1   Describe the women's visit to the tomb, as Mark told it.
2   Some manuscripts have a short ending to the Gospel following the 'longer ending'. Write it out.
3   Give three reasons why Mark may have ended his Gospel abruptly.
4   What did *Paul* have to say about the resurrection in his first letter to the Corinthians, chapter 15, verses 3–8?

C   Essays (Understanding & evaluation)
1   Outline the story of the women's visit to the tomb as Mark told it. Show how Mark's account differs from that of Luke. Comment on this.
2   Read Matthew's resurrection stories. Write an essay pointing out some of the differences between Matthew and Mark in their accounts of the resurrection. Do these differences present problems for the reader?
3   What *really* happened at the resurrection? Do Christians have to take the stories as literal descriptions of historical fact?
4   What evidence does Mark give for the resurrection of Jesus?

D   Things to do
1   Make a collage called 'resurrection'.
2   Everyone in the group/class ask a Christian to write down in a few words what he or she understands by the resurrection of Jesus. Compare all the answers.
3   Tell your group a resurrection story, where love and understanding triumph over hatred or fear.
4   Collect stories which have a resurrection theme from folk-lore or other world religions. (Don't overlook children's books.)
5   Either write a poem called 'From death to life'; or illustrate the theme in any artistic medium.

B9 Characteristics of Mark's Gospel

The Way In

Two people are invited to talk to a group about the Third World. One of them reads up everything he can lay his hands on, to make sure his presentation is completely accurate. Facts, figures and statistics are important to him, because he wants above all to present a true picture. He arranges his material most carefully, so that his audience will understand the situation as clearly as he does himself.

Here are the notes for his talk.

Talk on Colombia

1. Position of Colombia in S. America. Geography : show MAP
   Andes. Caribbean coast etc. mention VOLCANO disaster of 1986.

2. History. Spanish invasion in 16ᵗʰ. Spanish settlements
   eg. Santa Marta (1525) and Cartagena (1533)
          show pictures of Colonial style buildings.

3. Later history. Simon Bolivar & 'liberation' from Spain. 1819.
   Colombian Union (Venezuela, Ecuador & Colombia)   1820 - 30.

4. Present political position.   mention recent troubles cuttings.

5. Wealth of Colombia.   GOLD (NB. Gold Museum)
                          EMERALDS
                          COFFEE etc.

6. BOGOTÁ.   Show pictures of modern city and shanty towns.
          nb. Wealth versus Poverty.

7. Industry   around Medellin.

8. Flourishing trade in ~~marijuana~~ marijuana and cocaine. Santa Marta
   and the North.   (NB. economy depends on it).

9. A look at the Indian people. Take CHIBCHAS of
   Cundinamarca as the example.
      (a) History.   note violent Spanish conquest. / church
      (b) Life-style - then & now.
      (c) Mythology.   Bochica, Chibchachum etc.
      (d) Poverty & injustice.
   Conclude   with music of Indian people and show their crafts etc.

The other speaker also wants her audience to understand, and has done the same amount of research. But she decides to say little, and to let a series of coloured slides speak for themselves. Her presentation is apparently less orderly: slide after slide appears on the screen, in apparently haphazard order. But the impact is deep. Only afterwards does her audience realize how carefully and deliberately those slides had been chosen.

Mark's approach to the story of Jesus is more like the second presentation than the first.

Main Issues

Brilliant style

Mark is a brilliant writer. You need to read a piece of his Gospel in parallel columns with the other Gospels, and compare each line word by word, in order to realize what a vivid writer he is. Let's take the story of Jesus and the children, as an example.

Mark 10	Matthew 19	Luke 18
Some people brought children to Jesus for him to place his hands on them,	Some people brought children to Jesus for him to place his hands on them, and to pray for them,	Some people brought children to Jesus for him to place his hands on them,
but the disciples scolded the people. When Jesus noticed this, *he was angry* and said to his disciples, 'Let the children come to me, and do not stop them, because the Kingdom of God belongs to such as these. I assure you that whosoever does not receive the Kingdom of God like a child will never enter it.' Then he *took the children in his arms*, placed his hands on *each* of them, *and blessed them.*	but the disciples scolded the people. Jesus said 'Let the children come to me and do not stop them, because the Kingdom of heaven belongs to such as these.' He placed his hands on them and then went away.	The disciples saw them and scolded them for doing so. but Jesus called the children to him and said, 'Let the children come to me and do not stop them, because the Kingdom of God belongs to such as these. Remember this! Whosoever does not receive the Kingdom of God like a child will never enter it.'

Notice Mark's special touch—Jesus anger, Jesus embracing the children and pronouncing a blessing on them. Matthew and Luke, who wrote with a copy of Mark in front of them, chose to leave these phrases out. Their Gospels are never as brilliant in language as Mark's.

It is the same in story after story. Mark gives us the feeling of actually being present at the scene, of hearing the actual words spoken by Jesus in the original Aramaic—*Ephphata, Talitha Cum, Abba.*

Some scholars think that these extra little touches, the details of everyday life, are the memories of Peter, who passed them on to Mark. He tells his stories in the rather disjointed, disorderly way that stories are shared amongst friends. He gets his tenses muddled up—'so this man comes up and says to Jesus . . .'

Mark gives extra bits of detail which are quite irrelevant to the story, but which bring it to life—the pillow in the stern of the boat (4: 38), the crowds sitting down on the green grass (in the Greek it says they were grouped as 'flowerbeds' on the green grass, 6: 39–40) the whiteness of the Transfiguration 'whiter than anyone in the world could wash them' (9: 3).

Mark probably needs to be read in an accent or a dialect to get the flavour. Matthew and Luke, when they followed him, found him altogether too blunt and colloquial to copy word for word; their version of the Gospel story is more polished. Translators never dare to render the words exactly as he wrote because it wouldn't read as good English. He wrote in a very rough Greek.

By having unfinished sentences and a breathless pace, Mark presents a vivid and haphazard succession of scenes from the life of Jesus. They are thrown up at the reader like a series of slides on a screen. There isn't very much of Jesus' preaching—that all comes in the other three Gospels. For Mark, Jesus preaches by what he *is* and what he *does*.

The Gospel Theme

Mark was not writing a biography of Jesus. He announces in his opening line what the theme of his Gospel is going to be: '*This is the Good News about Jesus Christ, the Son of God.*' In this Gospel, this title 'Son of God' (which crops up frequently in the pages of Matthew and Luke), is not given again to Jesus until the last page. Voices from heaven (9: 7) and voices from hell (5: 7) proclaim him as God's son, but no human being does so until Jesus dies on the cross—only eight verses before the end of the story.

This is Mark's *mystery* or *secret*. The title 'Son of God' is difficult to understand. Mark says you have to wait till the end of the story before you really understand what it means. He underlines the mystery by having people ask again and again, 'Who is this?'.

People are constantly amazed at Jesus. They keep on misunderstanding him. According to Mark, Jesus keeps telling people not to reveal who he is. What did this theme of mystery and secretiveness really mean to Mark? Three answers are possible:

1 The secret is *factual*. Jesus was in fact secretive about claiming to be Messiah-Christ. For most people, the word had crude political over-tones which he repudiated. It was only slowly that he openly admitted to the title, after explaining the sort of Messiah he claimed to be.

2 The secret is *fictional*. Jesus was quite open about claiming to be Messiah-Christ. Yet the fact is that few people acknowledged him as such, least of all the Jews who longed for the Messiah. Embarrassed by this, the early Church 'explained' the scandal by pretending Jesus never claimed to be Messiah in public. He only told a few chosen friends in private.

3 The secret is *theological*. It is Mark's own deliberate device to explain what following Jesus really means. To follow Jesus and enthusiasti-cally call him Messiah-Christ—Son of God, simply because you like his teaching, or marvel at his healing powers, is to fail to accept him for what he truly is. The Son of God will be crucified. That is exactly what our world has always done to those who remain faithful to God. If Jesus had not suffered and died, it would have proved he was not the Son of God.

The death of Jesus, therefore is part of his task. He can't be called Son of God till he is on the cross. To blurt out the title too soon would obscure the real truth about him. Nor can his followers understand what being a Son of God is all about until the end of the story.

If this last explanation is correct, then Mark's is a stern Gospel. Written for a persecuted minority, it has always had a strong appeal for Christians who have to suffer for their faith, and perhaps always caused embarrassment to those whose Christianity has not interfered over-much with their peace, comfort and affluence.

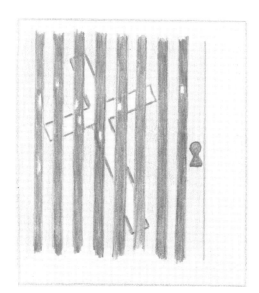

If you were accused of being a Christian would there be enough evidence to convict you?

Looking Deeper

Order in Mark's Gospel

Most scholars agree that of the four Gospels now existing, Mark's was the first to be written. Is Mark, therefore, likely to be the most accurate in recording the actual events of Jesus' life? Did he exactly record the words of Jesus? Is the story he tells in the correct chronological order? These questions have teased the scholars for centuries. There are various possibilities regarding the order in which Mark wrote:

1 No order at all;
2 Chronological order;
3 Practical order.

1　No order at all

Although the stories are set in a general chronological order (beginning with ministry first, death last), they are otherwise totally random. The first witness to the Gospel, Papias in the early 2nd century, described it as the memoirs of Peter, as they occurred to him, in no particular order. This suggests that Mark's Gospel is entirely haphazard.

2　Chronological order

Over the centuries, Papias' description was ignored. Since Mark had connected his stories into a narrative, he was presumed to have recorded the doings and sayings of Jesus in the right chronological order. The Gospel looked like a biography, so that was how it was read. This approach was never really questioned until the 20th century.

3　Practical order

Early this century, several German scholars looked more closely at the stories in Mark. They found that there was no real connection between the stories. They were all self-contained and easily interchangeable. Presumably they existed singly before Mark strung them together with 'ands' and 'thens'. Was it possible to tell, from their shape or *form* they asked, how these stories had grown up in the first place? This would tell us something of their purpose and meaning.

The *form-critics* (as the scholars were known) concluded that there was, after all, some order in Mark's Gospel. It was not a chronological order, because none of the stories had a date attached, but a practical order. These disconnected stories were carefully put together to teach something, that is, to illustrate who Mark understood Jesus to be. This means that we can no longer draw any strictly historical conclusions about Jesus from Mark's Gospel—what exactly happened and in what order. But we know a great deal from his Gospel about how the early Church interpreted the meaning of Jesus' life.

A Short answers (Knowledge)

1 Give *one* Aramaic word used by Mark in the Gospel.

2 For whom did Mark write his Gospel?

3 How does the Gospel begin? (Verse 1.)

4 In what language did Mark write?

5 When does Mark use the title 'Son of God' in the Gospel?

6 Luke's Gospel ends on a note of joy. On what note does Mark's Gospel end?

7 Which of the Apostles is said to have influenced Mark?

8 Which is the more polished Gospel, Mark or Matthew?

9 How would you describe Mark's style of writing?

10 How many times in the Gospel is Jesus misunderstood by his disciples?

B Longer answers (Knowledge & understanding)

1 Give two examples of Mark's writing where his vivid, colourful style is at its best.

2 Give three examples of people being seized with fear in the presence of Jesus.

3 Describe the scene at the death of Jesus where he is proclaimed 'Son of God'.

4 Give two examples from Mark where Jesus calls himself the Son of Man.

C Essays (Understanding & evaluation)

1 Mark's Gospel is not a biography of Jesus. So what is it?

2 'The three other Gospels are never as brilliant in language as Mark's.' Comment on this, using comparisons from the Gospels to show Mark's style of writing.

3 What according to Mark is the Messianic secret (or the mystery about Jesus)? Why does Mark present Jesus as secretive? Give examples from the text.

4 You have been asked to talk to a group of people about Mark's Gospel. They have never read it. What main points would you make to show them what is typical of Mark's Gospel. Illustrate your answer by referring to selected passages from the Gospel.

5 Show how *form-criticism* has had a big influence on how we now understand a Gospel.

6 On many occasions Mark comments that people were 'amazed' at Jesus. Describe briefly two of these occasions. Why were they so astounded?

D Things to do

1 Find out what you can about Roman persecutions of Christians around the year AD 65.

2 Take the headings of chapters B1–B7 (inclusive) as a guide and produce a seven-part frieze showing an outline of Mark's Gospel. Make it as colourful as possible.

3 Mark's stories seem to have been originally disconnected. Put them into a different order to see if you can make a different pattern.

B10   Who was Jesus?

'Christ' by Masaccio

Who do men say that I am?

1   *Who was the other who died on the hill?*
    Who was the other closed in for the kill?
    One was a robber and one was a thief—
    But who was the third man whose life was so brief?
        Who do men say that I am?
        Who do men say that I am?

2   *Some say a prophet come back from the dead,*
    Some—an idealist but rather misled;
    Some say a teacher, or King of the Jews,
    And some say God's son who had no power to choose.
        Who do men say . . .

3   *Some say a leader upholding the right,*
    Some say a rebel with no guts to fight;
    Some say a legend, and some say a fool,
    And some—an impostor just playing it cool.
        Who do men say . . .

4   *Who was the other who died on the hill?*
    Who was the other closed in for the kill?
    One was a robber and one was a thief—
    But who was the third man whose life was so brief?
        Who do men say . . .

Cecily Taylor ⓒ Stainer & Bell Ltd 1974

Who do you say that I am (Mark 8:29)

We need to return again to the scene described by Mark in chapter 8. Jesus is aware that people are talking about him and wants to know what they are saying. He then puts the crunch question to the disciples. Who do *you* say that I am? Peter speaks up on behalf of the others. He makes an impressive profession of faith, calling Jesus the Messiah (Christ).

Messiah is only one of the titles Jesus was given. There are others. We need to look at them.

1   Messiah (Hebrew) or Christ (Greek)

> *Peter answered, 'You are the Messiah'*   (Mark 8:29)

The word means 'anointed' (by God), in the sense of being singled out for a particular task. In the Old Testament all the kings of Israel were regarded as messiahs. When the monarchy died out, the word was kept as a title for the future king who, it was hoped (and many Jews still hope) would one day restore Israel's glory. The New Testament is convinced Jesus fulfilled these hopes, and applies the title so naturally to Jesus that it almost becomes his surname. Jesus is no longer 'the Christ', but simply 'Jesus Christ'.

2 Son of God

> *This is the Good News about Jesus Christ, the Son of God.* (Mark 1:1)

Mark puts the two titles side by side because they are closely connected. The Israelite king was seen as the adopted 'son' of God, the visible deputy for the invisible God. So he was enthroned, like a royal son, at the 'right hand' (south) of the Temple, but knew that he was only standing in for God.

3 Son of Man

> *Then the Son of Man will appear, coming in the clouds with great power and glory.* (Mark 13:43)

This title which sounds so utterly human, is strangely far more 'divine' than the title 'Son of God'. It comes from the book of Daniel (7:13. NB The Good News Bible translates it as 'human being'), where it stands for a humane Israel which, it was hoped, would eventually *ascend on a cloud* to God to be crowned, and so replace all the brutish empires that had ruled the world so far. Later writers turned this 'Son of Man' symbol into an actual heavenly person, hardly distinguishable from God. He, it was hoped, would finally *descend on a cloud* from heaven, and announce the Kingdom. The Gospel writers identified this heavenly person with Jesus. (See Mark 8:38, 13:26, 14:62.)

4 Suffering Servant of God

> *For even the Son of Man did not come to be served; he came to serve.* (Mark 10:45)

The task of Israel and above all of its representative the king, was to obey God, to be his servant. This could involve pain and suffering. The book of Isaiah speaks of the ideal Israel as a suffering servant. Four great poems (chapters 42–53) outline the persecution which the one so chosen must undergo. But his reward is vindication by God and glorious exaltation. The Evangelists saw Jesus as this ideal Israel. Mark is particularly sensitive to this suffering role.

5 Lord

> *And if someone asks you why you are doing that, tell him that the Master (Lord) needs it.* (Mark 11:3)

The title 'Lord' (Kyrios) has a 'low' meaning and a 'high' meaning. Mark uses it of Jesus only twice, and it is correctly translated as 'Master' (11:3) or 'Sir' (7:28). Both texts seem to use the word in the 'low' sense as a simple courtesy title. But it was also used in a 'high' sense, particularly in the Old Testament, where 'Lord' regularly stands for the name of God himself, Yahweh. This high meaning of the title was thought to be most appropriately applied to Jesus after the resurrection (though Luke happily gives Jesus this title throughout his Gospel). In Mark it is to be found only in the appendix 16:19–20.

What did the New Testament think about Jesus?

There are other titles given to Jesus in the New Testament. The ones we have examined tell us very clearly what its writers thought about Jesus. For them, he was the long awaited Messiah (Christ),
>   the royal Son standing in for God,
>   the heavenly Son of Man,
>   the ideal Israel who suffered to serve God,
>   even the Divine Lord himself.
When people write in such superlative terms, they presumably have reason for doing so.

> *It would have been ridiculous had the disciples, after the resurrection, attributed Lordship and mastery of death to a kind of Nazareth mouse who had hardly squeaked in his lifetime.*
>
> Peter De Rosa *Jesus Who Became Christ*

It is probable that the New Testament writers' assessment of Jesus is at least fair comment. Presumably what they had seen in Jesus and heard from him entitled them to speak of him in such glowing terms. Would Jesus agree?

Would Jesus agree?

This is a harder question to answer. The New Testament titles tell us clearly what Jesus' disciples thought of him. They tell us nothing about what Jesus thought of himself.

Would he happily have accepted such high-flown titles? Tim Rice, in a still popular musical, poses the same question:

> *Jesus Christ, Superstar,*
> *Do you think you're what they say you are?*

There is, in fact, no evidence that Jesus ever claimed these titles for himself. All the evidence points in the opposite direction.

1   He refused to be equated with God ('*Why do you call me good? No one is good except God alone.*' Mark 10:18. Matthew will soften this saying.)
2   He seems at times to have refused to accept the title of Messiah-Christ: it had political overtones which he wanted nothing to do with (see Mark 8:30, 15:2).
3   For him, the very title 'Son of Man' probably had no divine overtone and meant no more than 'I myself'.
4   The Gospels sometimes give the impression that he preached about himself. In fact, he constantly pointed away from himself to God. It was God's Rule he proclaimed not his own.

So who was he?

This may suggest we no longer know much about Jesus—only about his disciples' enthusiastic claims for him. But this would be too pessimistic. Through those Christian claims, we actually know a lot about Jesus. Who must he have been, that he was able to convince them that he spoke on behalf of God and that in his ministry the Rule of God had come to earth? The constant experience of Christians has been that here is someone uniquely related to God, someone who reveals the face of a God otherwise hidden.

How do Christians express this unique relationship of Jesus to God? In two ways.

1   Some start at the 'God-end'. If Jesus is so at one with God, then he is what God is: eternal, infinite, unlimited, sinless, all powerful, all present, all knowing, unchangeable. In this view, there are no problems about the stories of his virginal birth, his miracles and his resurrection. It is what one would expect.

2   Some Christians today find such talk unhelpful. They feel that it not only presumes we know exactly what God is (we don't), but also that it makes Jesus so remote that many people never get on his wavelength. These Christians prefer to start with Jesus the man, a Jew of the 1st century, who is no less human than the rest of us, but more so, living the same human life that all people do, and limited in every way by ignorance, darkness and doubt. Stories which seem to place him safely outside our human condition (virginal birth, miracles, resurrection) may need to be taken less literally than they once were. Nevertheless they remain powerful poetic expressions of what Jesus means to the believer, the *God-send* who transforms their lives because he lives on even after he died.

Both sorts of Christians claim to know what God is like by looking at the man Jesus. In an utterly human life they claim to see, undistorted, the face of God. Everyone reading the Gospel is invited to consider Jesus' question:

'Who do you *say that I am?'*

A 1 Read the following passage and answer the questions that follow.

They came to Jericho, and as Jesus was leaving with his disciples and a large crowd, a blind beggar named Bartimaeus son of Timaeus was sitting by the road. When he heard that it was Jesus of Nazareth he began to shout, 'Jesus! Son of David! take pity on me!'

Many of the people scolded him and told him to be quiet. But he shouted even more loudly, 'Son of David, take pity on me!'

Jesus stopped and said, 'Call him.'

So they called the blind man. 'Cheer up!' they said. 'Get up, he is calling you.'

He threw off his cloak, jumped up, and came to Jesus.

'What do you want me to do for you?' Jesus asked him.

'Teacher,' the blind man answered, 'I want to see again.'

'Go,' Jesus told him, 'your faith has made you well.'

At once he was able to see and followed Jesus on the road.

(a) Who was David?

(b) This is the last healing story in Mark's Gospel. Describe very briefly another healing story.

(c) Whereabouts in the Gospel does this story appear? Has Mark placed it in his text with care? Comment.

(d) Jesus heals Bartimaeus because of his *faith*. Give an example from modern life where you think someone shows faith.

(e) Mark has another 'blind man' story in chapter 8. Between these two healing stories Mark includes a number of incidents which comment on discipleship. Pick out two such incidents and describe them.

(f) This story was probably used in the early church as a good example of discipleship. What does it mean to be a disciple of Jesus today?

2 Read the following passage and answer the questions below.

This is the Good News about Jesus Christ, the Son of God. It began as the prophet Isaiah had written:
'God said, "I will send my messenger ahead of you to clear the way for you."
Someone is shouting in the desert,
"Get the road ready for the Lord; make a straight path for him to travel!"'

(a) The word *Christ* is Greek. What is its equivalent in Hebrew?

(b) What does the word *Christ* mean?

(c) Who was the messenger preparing the way for Jesus?

(d) Describe briefly the three short sections of this prologue.

(e) Mark says here that Jesus is the *Son of God*. That title will be acknowledged by a human being only once more in the Gospel. By whom, when, and why?

(f) In Mark's Gospel Jesus seems to hide his identity. What do you understand by this theme of secrecy?

(g) *'To say Jesus is God is easy. To accept it is difficult. To live out its implications is crucifying.'* (See page 74.) Would you say this is true for Christians today?

B **A few questions to get you thinking**

1 If Jesus' life was so impressive, why didn't more people follow him?

2 Christians say 'Jesus is alive today'. Where is he?

3 If God, through Jesus, *could* cure the sick and feed the hungry, why is there so much sickness and hunger in the world today?

4 *'Where does the Church come in? I can follow the example of Jesus without going to church.'* Comment.

Part C

─────Mark for Today─────

Living in the shadow of the cross

Mark for today

This section is a kind of anthology, a collage of ideas. It is intended as a jumping-off point for discussions, group work or course work. There are many topics of importance and interest missing from this selection, for example, prayer, ecumenism, authority etc. Students interested in these or other topics would do well to prepare their own outline sheets on the model suggested in this book. These could serve as outlines for more detailed projects or course work.

We live in a complex world. Natural resources are being used up by the industrial nations, at such a rate that the very future looks uncertain. Every day sees the gap widening between the rich and poor nations. The advent of micro-technology only heightens the prospect of increasing unemployment. Violence and crime are on the increase. Nuclear weapons continue to be stockpiled, and reactor accidents continue to make the headlines, so that many people fear that a nuclear disaster is imminent. Improved medicine allows people to live longer, and so creates a population problem. Meanwhile wars continue, many of them rooted in religious intolerance.

What has Mark's Gospel to say about a world like this?

1   We should not expect the Gospels to give us any immediate answer to today's problems. Many of them did not exist in the time of Jesus. Equally, neither do many of us have to face the problem that faced Mark's first readers.

2   However, the judgement that the Gospels pass on their world is based on certain *principles*, and these principles are not tied down to one age. Christians believe that the Gospels are for all time. In each of the following sections, readers are invited to try to trace the principles on which Christians today make their judgements.

3   Jesus urged people to ask questions about the world they lived in, and to make up their own minds, even if it got them into trouble with authority. Mark is particularly keen to show that being a follower of Jesus is no bed of roses. The following pages will illustrate this.

4   There are no easy answers to the world's problems. There are Christians who stand, firmly convinced, on both sides of most arguments.

C1 Home and family

Ideal of Marriage

> *No man is an Island,*
> *entire of itself.*

Probably everyone knows this quotation from John Donne. It means that we need one another. We are only complete when we communicate with others. Our relationship with others is the most important aspect of our lives.

Why are TV soap operas so popular, sometimes to the point of addiction? Presumably because they continually analyse these relationships. And when they concentrate on the marriage relationship, audience viewing shoots up by millions.

The most important relationship which most people will enter into, is marriage.

What is marriage?

Marriage is the binding union of a man and a woman who commit themselves to each other for life. It has existed in all societies and all cultures from time immemorial, which suggests that it is part of human nature to enter such a binding relationship. All religions see marriage as something sacred.

Judaism and Christianity speak of marriage as something designed by God. The Genesis story of Adam and Eve is a joyful comment on the happiness of marriage, and describes it as a gift from God. And when Jesus was questioned about marriage, he referred his questioners (says Mark) to the Genesis text:

> *God made them male and female ... And for that reason a man will leave his father and mother and unite with his wife, and the two will become one ...'*
>
> Mark 10: 6

Family life has always been important in Judaism and in Christianity. The lifelong commitment is taken very seriously, since only marriage is seen as able to provide the secure social framework within which children are born most happily. Indeed, since sexual intercourse is understood as a profound symbol of the unity now existing between the two partners, sex outside marriage is forbidden.

All societies celebrate marriage with a solemn ritual. The Church of England sees the marriage vows as made 'in the name of God'.

Roman Catholics think so highly of marriage that they call it a *sacrament*, that is, a visible sign of the presence of God. The love between husband and wife is seen as reflecting and expressing the love relation between God and the world, between Christ and the Church.

Questions and tasks

1   Choose a current TV soap opera which everyone in the class can watch for 2 or 3 episodes. Then have a discussion about the relationships it portrays.

2   You know the question 'Which comes first, the chicken or the egg?' In which order would you put the following: marriage, love, sex?
    Say why.

3   Study the marriage service of a Christian church.

There is a Russian proverb which says: '*Love is a glass which shatters if you hold it too tightly, or too loosely.*' If the loving relationship we have with another person is the most important and precious aspect of our lives, it is also the most delicate and vulnerable. Relationships are easily broken.

Don't talk of love;
I've heard the word before;
It's sleeping in my memory
And I won't disturb the slumber
Of feelings that have died.
If I never loved I never would have cried.
I am a rock, I am an island.
                                        Paul Simon

Love involves sacrifice. It is about sharing, trust, responsibility, empathy, caring, forgiveness, generosity, tolerance. The list could go on. It is no wonder that married life is not easy.

Christians believe that the presence of God in their marriage can enable them to work together to overcome the difficulties they encounter. They are inspired by the person of Jesus whose love involved the ultimate sacrifice of his own life. Mark reminded his contemporaries that they couldn't expect to call themselves Christians without a similar painful experience. (See page 74.)

> *All marriages are happy. It's the living together afterwards that causes all the trouble.*
>
> Farmers' Almanac

Today's society can put enormous strains on relationships. Unemployment, for example, can have a devastating effect on a family. Marriages have been wrecked because of it.

• What other social pressures are causing almost unbearable strain on married life?

The State allows for marriages to break down and *divorce* is legally permissible. But the Christian Churches hesitate to approve of it, mindful of Jesus' teaching:

> *Man must not separate, then, what God has joined together.*
> Mark 10:9

The Roman Catholic Church does not allow any form of divorce with remarriage. It has an *annulment* procedure where a couple may be released from a union which on examination is deemed to have been invalid.

Until recently the Church of England did not allow remarriage after divorce. This is changing.

> *Let there be spaces in your togetherness.*
> Kahlil Gibran

Questions and tasks

1   Discuss the argument: 'We need to live together before we get married to see if we are suited.'

2   Many letters to Agony Aunts relate to love, sex, marriage. Find some of these in magazines and write down your own answers to the questions. Compare these with one another.

3   The Gospel presents a Jesus who is both clear in his teaching about the permanence of marriage, but compassionate to people who struggle and fail. How then can Christians follow his example in relation to divorce?

Respect For Life

when I grow up I shall have lots of babis, Then I'll get married and live happily ever after.   lisa aged 6.

We hope she will. The fact that the majority of young people will eventually marry and have a family indicates that it remains a most satisfying and fulfilling way of life.

Psychologists and psychiatrists will verify that damaged, sick people often come from broken, unhappy homes. Happy, mature and balanced people can usually look back on a secure childhood. (There are, of course, exceptions.) It is obvious that the stability and happiness of family life is of fundamental importance.

> *The family may be regarded as the cradle of civil society, and it is in great measure within the circle of family life that the destiny of states is fostered.*
>
> Pope Leo XIII

Often we read cynical descriptions of the 'happy home'.

> *Freud is all nonsense; the secret neurosis is to be found in the family battle of wills to see who can refuse longest to help with the dishes. The sink is the great symbol of the bloodiness of family life. All life is bad, but family life is worse.*
>
> Julian Mitchell *As Far as You Can Go*

There are plenty of remarks made like this and many cynical cartoons. But it remains a fact that most couples want a family and some will go to any lengths to have children.

Christians celebrate the gift of *life* in the sacrament of *baptism*. For all Christian Churches it is the welcoming of a new member (usually an infant) into the wider family community of the Church.

Married couples have to make many decisions. In today's society this can be difficult. Modern medical science has been able to solve some of their difficulties, but has in its turn created a number of ethical problems.

Many people, for example, find the *test-tube* baby programme morally unacceptable. They include some Christians. Why?

• Find out more about the arguments for and against embryo research.

The Churches hold differing views about *family planning*. The Roman Catholic Church officially forbids all forms of contraception except 'natural' methods of planning. Why? What is natural?

The Churches are more united in their opposition to *abortion*. Christians believe that the life of a child before birth is as sacred as that of a child after birth.

• Discuss how pre-birth screening (scanning, amniocentesis) presents parents with new difficulties.

The *adoption* and *fostering* of babies in this country has become difficult (with abortion and contraception available few babies are offered for adoption). New laws are going to make it impossible for cross-culture adoptions to take place in England. But overseas adoptions are on the increase.

• Do you think it is sensible to transfer children from one culture to another in this way?

Questions and tasks

1   If so many of these issues are created by today's society, how can the Christian Gospel have anything to say about them?
2   Write for information to LIFE; SPUC; Dr Barnardo's Homes; Diocesan Catholic Children's Homes; Local Adoption Agencies.

> *The one thing children wear out faster than shoes is parents.*
> John Plomp

> *He took the children in his arms, placed his hands on each of them, and blessed them.*
> Mark 10:16

> *The young people of today think of nothing but themselves. They have no reverence for parents or old age. They talk as if they knew everything. As for girls, they are immodest and unwomanly in speech, behaviour and dress.*
> Peter the Monk in AD 1274

> *What a mother sings to the cradle goes all the way down to the coffin.*
> Henry Ward Beecher
> 1887

> *One doctor said to another doctor:*
> *'About the termination of a pregnancy, I want your opinion. The father was a syphilic. The mother was tuberculous. Of the four children born, the first was blind, the second died, the third was deaf and dumb, the fourth also tuberculous. What would you have done?'*
> *'I would have ended the pregnancy.'*
> *'Then you would have murdered Beethoven.'*
> Maurice Baring

C2 God, Christianity and mission

God

Jews, Christians and Muslims worship the One God. Who is God?
What a difficult question!
Attempts to define God fall into three styles:

1 Concrete 'images'. For example, the Jewish and Christian image of God as a loving Father.
2 Abstract descriptions. For example, the revelation to Moses (Exodus 3:14) '*I am who I am*'.
3 Mystical experience where words are totally inadequate. Some people will tell you that they *know* God exists, from their deep, personal experience. But they find it impossible even to attempt a definition. Quakers, for example, believe in God but make no dogmatic attempts to define the reality.

God is dancing because no one is being naughty.

• How would you define God?

Here are some descriptions of God taken from a recent adult survey:

'A white-haired elderly man with a smiling face.'
'An indulgent parent.'
'Jesus is God in human form.'
'A friend whom I can always approach.'
'An all-pervading Spirit in the cosmos.'
'A mystery that will be revealed when I die.'
'A mother giving birth to all creation and a father who disciplines.'

God, Jesus and Mark

In this book we have seen how Jesus understood the word 'God'. He preached about it and was put to death for his views. His followers were quick to see that Jesus' understanding of God was rooted in his *unique* relationship with God. He was the 'Son of God'. Mark wrote his Gospel to express his belief in this unique relationship. '*This man was really the Son of God.*' (Mark 15:39.)
Christians are those who share Mark's belief.

Christian Worship

The natural response to belief in God is faith and worship. In its normal use today, Christian 'worship' refers to the community gathered together to express its adoration, praise and thanksgiving to God through Christ.
From the earliest times people were chosen to lead the community in worship. This position of leadership (bishop, elder, priest) has always been regarded as an important one.

> In the Roman Catholic Church ordination to the priesthood is described as one of the *sacraments*. *'By the sacrament of Ministry particular members of the community are ordained to share in a special (sacramental) way in the priesthood of the Church which is the priesthood of Christ.'*
>
> Herbert McCabe OP

Authority in the Church

Authority is a tricky subject. It is not easy to know what kind of structure will best help a community survive and grow. Jesus himself would probably find it difficult to recognize the *Church structures* which eventually emerged. But some structure there had to be.

● Find out all you can about the organization and authority structures in different Christian Churches. Who is in charge of what?

The word 'minister' means servant. Ministers are chosen to be at the *service* of the people. Even the Pope calls himself the 'Servant of the servants of God.'

● In what way does your local minister, vicar or priest serve the community?
● How do bishops serve the people?

In the Roman Catholic Church priests are required to remain celibate. Some ministers of other Churches also choose celibacy, believing that it allows for greater freedom in working for others. Some men and women choose to live a celibate life in community.

In the past spiritual writers treated celibacy and religious life as a 'higher calling', thus creating two classes of Christians. Today's theologians emphasize that *all* baptized people are called to live the Gospel. Priests, religious and 'lay' Christians, single or married, have the same responsibility to live lives of commitment.

Ask a local nun or monk to come and talk about their life and work.

> 'Beware of the man whose God is in the skies.'
> Bernard Shaw

> 'If God did not exist, it would be necessary to invent him.'
> Voltaire

> 'God often visits us, but most of the time we are not at home.'
> French proverb

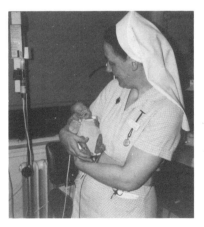

A Roman Catholic nun working in a special care unit

Brother Keith, an Anglican monk, is led away from a CND demonstration

Questions and tasks

1   '*I thank God for the death of God . . . it has allowed the* real *God to appear.*' (H J Richards.) Some of the old concepts of God have 'gone dead' on people. What ideas of God would you reject, and why?

2   Invite leaders from the local churches to come and tell you about their role in the Church.

3   '*Why can't women be ordained priests?*' Find out all you can about the current controversy over women priests. What do you think about it?

Love and Service of Others

Compassion for the millions who suffer hunger and disease inspires many people to lives of service for them. This is a natural enough humanitarian response to need. For Christians it is also a response to their Christian vocation. What does that mean?

A British nun at a Peruvian mission

The life of Jesus was one of total service to others. To be his *follower* implies a life of giving and caring. When Jesus was asked which was the most important commandment, he replied:

> '*Love the Lord your God with all your heart, with all your soul, with all your mind, and with all your strength.*' *The second most important commandment is this: '*Love your neighbour as you love yourself.*' There is no other commandment more important that these two.*
>
> Mark 12 : 30–31

Mark is at pains in his Gospel to show that this is no easy option. It demands a selflessness that approaches martyrdom.

> To be at the service of others is part of the vocation of all Christians in virtue of their baptism. But since many Christians are baptized as infants, this commitment is 'confirmed' as they enter adulthood. Anglican, Orthodox and Roman Catholic Christians speak of this as their *confirmation*. For Roman Catholics it is one of the seven sacraments. Some of the Free Churches speak of it simply as 'Becoming a Member'.

Mr Terry Waite, a prominent Anglican layman

Cliff Richard at a Tear Fund project in Kenya

Lay Ministries in the Churches

To be a fully-grown member of the Church involves serving others, as has been said. But it involves taking on responsibility. Lay people do not simply 'belong' to the Church. They *are* the Church.

In the *Anglican Church* the laity have an official role, even in government. However in the *Roman Catholic Church* the role of the laity has only been brought to the fore since the Second Vatican Council (1963–65).

By contrast the *United Reformed Church*, and some other Free Churches, have no hierarchical structures; all the members share in the one priesthood and therefore have shared responsibility for decisions.

• Find out about the role of the laity in one Christian Church. Don't all choose the same denomination.

It is not surprising that many of the caring agencies in this country were founded by Christians.

Oxfam was founded in World War II by the Quakers;
Christian Aid in 1946 by the British Council of Churches;
CAFOD in 1962 by the Roman Catholic Church;
Tear Fund in 1968 by the Interdenominational Evangelical Alliance;
The Samaritans in 1953 by an Anglican priest.

• Find out more about one of the above agencies.

'The Christian's faith teaches him to use all things, including his money, responsibly. He seeks to meet problems and stresses by following Christ's teaching and living by his power. To Christ he offers the undiminished vigour of his body and mind. He loves his neighbour and therefore examines the probable effect of his behaviour, his habits and his example upon his neighbour. He accepts his part in the responsibility of the Church in the way of education and rehabilitation.'
The Methodist Church

• How can Christians demand such generosity from themselves, and yet be totally accepting of those who fail to show any generosity? Do they demand too much of themselves? Or do they simply like to feel superior? Or what? Discuss.

C3 Work, wealth and leisure

Work

Everyone needs to work. When people are unemployed, they feel frustrated, and bored.

Yet there is an ambiguity about work. At times it brings joy and a sense of fulfilment. At other times it is felt as a burden, more boring even than unemployment.

Look at these photographs:

We work to produce the goods we need for survival in the kind of world we have made for ourselves. In earlier days, a great deal of human work was associated with the land. Communities were small and transport between them was not very good. So families tended mainly to provide for their own needs (photo 1).

1

The industrial revolution made mass production possible. Work took on a completely different nature (photo 2).

Today we are experiencing an electronic revolution. The microchip, although it creates many new jobs in technology, is taking away many more jobs, even of skilled workers (photo 3).

Christian attitudes to work

Christians generally regard their work as an essential part of Christian living. If Christians can only love God by loving others, then every job is important because it is at the service of others.

In the 16th century, the Christian leader, John Calvin, developed this idea and concluded that hard work was a passport to salvation. From this emerged a 'work ethic' in which some sociologists see the beginnings of the system known as *capitalism*.

Karl Marx reacted strongly against this (Protestant) work ethic, and out of his protest *communism* was born.

2

- Find out more about these opposing ideas on work.

Compare these remarks made by a random selection of people.

'Well my work is boring. I have to do it to earn the money I want to spend on myself and on girls.'

'I love my work. We all have a laugh together and at the end of the day, I know we are doing something useful for other people.'

'I don't like my job. It pays well though and is a good stepping stone to a really important position in management.'

'I work at home. Well, I look after the family first, of course. But I make children's clothes to sell. I love it because I design them myself.'

What would be your ideal job?

> *'I like work. It fascinates me. I can sit and look at it for hours.'*
> Jerome K Jerome

> *'How many people work in the Vatican City, Holy Father?'*
> *'About half.'*
> Story told of
> Pope John XXIII

3

Work problems

1 Conscience

Life was simple when work was family-based. Today, when people have to work in industry or the professions, they have to make difficult decisions.

Could you work at a nuclear plant knowing that a mistake could cause untold disasters to human beings?

Could you work in a factory which produces armaments which could kill millions?

Could you accept a job which you suspect requires some dishonesty in practice?

Could you work in the medical profession at a job which requires decisions about life and death?

Could you accept a big pay rise which puts other people on the dole?

Could you work in the law profession which may mean defending the indefensible or condemning the innocent?

● Hold a class/group debate for and against taking these hypothetical jobs.

The questions illustrate the responsibility you take on as an adult. Christians are given some guidelines in the Gospel about the way they should live in relation to others. Some would say that these guidelines demand that they take radical decisions about their work, and that they refuse certain occupations.

> Jesus went to the Temple and began to drive out all those who were buying and selling. He overturned the tables of the money-changers and the stools of those who sold pigeons . . .
>
> Mark 11:15

2 Wealth

> Does a person gain anything if he wins the whole world but loses his life? Of course not.'
>
> Mark 8:34

According to Mark, Jesus makes it clear that pursuing a position or wealth in this world isn't worth very much. Everyone knows that the wealthiest people are not always the happiest.

We need money to provide necessities of life. In this country we are privileged with a Welfare System, where money is given to those who cannot work for it.

Look at the photos and the cutting in the margin and comment on the problems people can get into over money.

3 Unemployment

This is an enormous problem today. We are moving towards an age when there will not be enough jobs for everyone. This demands a radical reassessment of the way we live as a community. Have you any ideas about it?

Questions

1 What do you think about the idea of job-sharing?
2 *'Everyman's work, whether it be literature or music or pictures or architecture or anything else, is always a portrait of himself.'* (Samuel Butler 1835–1902.)

Is this true of the housewife and the factory worker?
3 Do you think the trade unions have too much or too little power?
4 Is it better to have a boring or distasteful job than none at all?
5 *'Those who have some means think that the most important thing in the world is love. The poor know that it is money.'* (Gerald Brenan)

Comment on this remark.

What is Leisure?

How do you spend your leisure time?

Most people associate leisure with enjoyment and relaxation. For some it is activity outside their 'paid employment'; for some it is actual physical work, but done for themselves—like building a garden shed.

Look at these photographs and discuss each one.

• Leisure is now an industry, participation costs money. Discuss the problems.

• Children learn from play: list everything that can be learnt by young children in this way.

• Shared leisure pursuits can help the handicapped to feel more accepted by the community. What is done about this in your area?

• Does the increased leisure time of the unemployed cause such boredom that people become destructive?

Questions

1   *'We need one day of the week for our leisure.'* Comment with reference to Sunday trading.
2   Is competition in sport healthy, or does it only reinforce failure for some people?
3   In this age of fewer jobs and longer life, leisure time is increasing. Does this prospect of extended leisure please you?

All Things in Moderation

Most people would agree that moderation makes sense. To live healthy and balanced lives, we need the challenge of work, plus some re-straining discipline on our lives, plus the freedom to choose activities which give us relaxation and pleasure. *'All work and no play makes Jack a dull boy.'* Christians, like other religious believers, hold that God is glorified by our 'wholeness'. Early in the 2nd century St Irenaeus wrote, *'The Glory of God is man (woman) fully alive.'*

For this wholeness we need time to ourselves—even though it appears to be 'selfish'. Jesus himself felt the pressure of life:

> *There were so many people coming and going that Jesus and his disciples didn't even have time to eat. So he said to them, 'Let us go off by ourselves to some place where we will be alone and you can rest for a while.' So they started out in a boat . . .*
>
> Mark 6: 31–32

Some people relax most easily alone. They go fishing, or walking, or do yoga. Others need company—a drink at the local, a vigorous game of squash, or an evening class in woodwork.

Some people don't feel happy unless their leisure time is spent in a constructive way. Is this a response to the Genesis command to be creative? Or is it a guilty hangover from the puritan Christianity which said that only *work* was pleasing to God; time spent socially was laziness and vanity.

> *For Satan finds some mischief still*
> *For idle hands to do.*
> Isaac Watts 1674–1748

In puritan households the only rest which people were allowed was on Sundays. This rest consisted of prayers and Bible readings. Today, the vast majority of Christians find such behaviour extreme, and ask whether it has anything to do with the Jesus of the Gospel.

● Did Jesus have a sense of humour? Give evidence for your answer.

C4 Crime and violence

Crime, Punishment and Forgiveness

In North America and Europe the crime rate goes up year by year. Our prisons are overcrowded and they are often tense and hostile places. Rising numbers of prisoners are on remand—as the queue waiting for trial lengthens.

• Why do people turn to crime. Is it boredom? greed? social inadequacy? There could be other causes. Name them.

In a recent television documentary on Holloway Prison it was stated that a few years ago the philosophy which inspired the building of the new prison was: *Prisoners are not bad, they are sad*. It seems that ten years later, this philosophy has been abandoned for lack of resources.

What is prison for? If prisoners are 'not bad' but 'sad', then their treatment should be sympathetic and healing. The Christian would identify this attitude with the way Jesus treated the 'sinners' of his day.

> *I have not come to call respectable people, but outcasts.*
>
> Mark 2:17

How do you see prison? Is it to:
(a) punish people;
(b) deter others from crime;
(c) to reform people?

Jesus' own life manifested the absolute forgiveness of a loving God. Forgiveness of sin is one of the key Christian doctrines.

> The Roman Catholic Church celebrates this aspect of God's love in what is known as the *sacrament* of penance (confession). From the earliest days the church based its claim to minister to sinners in this way on the authority of Jesus. He spoke on behalf of God and forgave sinners. The Church spoke for him.

> *'I will prove to you then, that the Son of Man has authority on earth to forgive sins.' So he said to the paralysed man, 'I tell you, get up, pick up your mat, and go home.'*
>
> Mark 2:10–11

Johnny Smith
Bereft of kith
Scarred his skin
Bereft of kin,
Bolted
Thieved
Slept rough
Was found.

Johnny rest
Breathe
Go on
Curse but don't
Yourself confound.

We're confused
Can't find a way
To help you
Understand and stay
Johnny stay.

Johnny kicked out of school
Told 'be good'
Don't play the fool
Told its up to you
To prove
Goodness can prevail
And love.
See the system demonstrate
Its own capacity
To hate.

Johnny Smith
Bereft of kith.

Nadine Brummer

This poem asks 'Who is the offender?'.

There are many people in prison throughout the world, for their political or religious beliefs. These prisoners of conscience are helped by *Amnesty International*.

Amnesty is independent of any government, ideology or creed.

11 held in soccer video swoops

By Ian Smith

Operation Unruly swung into action at dawn yesterday when police officers swooped on the homes of football supporters and arrested 13 people suspected of involvement in the Odsal football riot in P month. T...

calls, including many friends and relatives of t... arrested when they relea... their f... ...blic viewh... last F... Ca... susp... sho...

Horror at child rioters

..., social workers and ...s in North Belfast have ...horrified to find that a ...te of rioting in the area ...veloped from a clash be-...ween children aged between ...four and ten, from both sides of the religious divide.

The Catholics came mainly from the New Lodge area and their Loyalist counterparts from th... Protestant stronghold known ...er Bay... ...rience was describe' ...by Mrs Mc... ...orke...

IRA boy took guns to killers

A youth who was involved in the Provisional IRA mur-...der of a part-time soldier when ...was aged 13 was jailed for ...en years yesterday ...ul Smyth had b... ...lost road '...y'd in...

'Drink and crime' link

ALCOHOL abuse is still the main source of most crime and social problems in Scotland. ...the claim in the annual ...ector of Consta-...

Questions and tasks

1   Are there any types of criminal who should *never* be released? If you believe there are, does this mean that they are never forgiven?
2   Can a practising Christian support the death penalty? (A Christian believes that all life is sacred.)
3   Would you welcome an ex-prisoner into your family?
4   Invite a prison officer/probation officer to talk to your class/group.

Prejudice

Prejudice is the labelling of people as 'goodies or baddies,' and refusing to change the labels. Some groups are permanently despised and considered second-class because of prejudice.

There is no one who is not prejudiced for or against something or someone. Some flaw in our human nature makes us believe that we can only survive by doing down others. Even Jesus' own villagers turned against him because he didn't conform to their ideas—he was different.

Today no wall divides the Jews from the Christians in Jerusalem

'How does he perform miracles? Isn't he the carpenter; the son of Mary, and the brother of James, Joseph, Judas and Simon? Aren't his sisters living here?' And so they rejected him.

Mark 6: 2–3

Jesus himself made the outcasts of society his friends. Christians have, through the ages, tried to follow this example, and worked to overcome prejudice.

The extreme left and the extreme right are both tolerated in Britain. Should they be . . . ?

Yet in other ways Christians have been as guilty of prejudice and intolerance as any other group.

The Nazi persecution and slaughter of Jews in Germany was the result of centuries of Christian mistrust and contempt.

The apartheid system in South Africa was created by Christian Whites who believed that the Bible said they were superior to Blacks.

Violence

When people have been despised as second-class for a long time, or not been given what they regard as their rights, they may in frustration, rightly or wrongly, resort to violence.

Can anyone liberate me?

- Do you consider the IRA to be freedom-fighters or terrorists?

Liberation theology

Some Christians in Third World countries believe that justice will only come about by revolution. Some even maintain that violence may be needed, to overthrow the greater 'violence' of poverty and injustice.

This is a new and controversial issue in the Churches. How far should a Christian be political in action? Some say, not at all. Some say it is impossible to be a Christian without being political. What do you think? Is the Jesus of Mark's Gospel 'political'?

War

There is always a war going on somewhere in the world. Even where there is 'peace', there are constant threats of future wars in the ongoing struggle for power and superiority.

Nations don't trust each other. In today's world the build-up of nuclear arms has introduced an entirely new threat. A future war could wipe out the human race.

Christians take different positions on the subject of war.

Pacifists
Pacifists refuse to take military action against others. Some Christians say this was Jesus' way: non-resistance and forgiveness.

Just war
In the past, the Christian churches have claimed that there can be good reasons to fight a war:

> *Governments cannot be denied the right to legitimate defence once every means of peaceful settlement has been exhausted.*
> *Church in the Modern World* Document of Vatican II

Nuclear war
Given the stockpile of arms, it is more and more likely that the next major war will be a nuclear one. Some Christians believe it is necessary to possess nuclear weapons in order to *deter* others from using them. On the other hand, the Churches are speaking out more and more strongly against all nuclear arms, and many Christians are in the forefront of the campaign to ban them totally.

> *We have to affirm that violence is contrary to the Gospel, violence is not Christian.*
> Pope Paul VI

> *I am opposed to all forms of violence ... But I am aware, as a man of peace, that there may come a time ... when we will have to say that the lesser of the two evils is to overthrow this unjust system.*
> Archbishop Desmond Tutu 1985

> *The destructive power of modern warfare, with the nuclear threat at its core, faces mankind with an appalling fact—the continuation of the human race can no longer be taken for granted.*
> *The Storm That Threatens* Statement of the Irish Bishops

CND demonstration at Lakenhead

• Is God on anyone's side in a war?
• What is multilateral and unilateral disarmament? Prominent Christians speak out on both sides of the disarmament debate. How is this?
• Was Jesus a pacifist?

C5　World problems

Poverty

We live in a world where wealth is unevenly and unfairly distributed. Two-thirds of our world goes hungry.

We belong to the rich one-third. The rich section, called the *First World*, includes North America, Europe, Japan, Australia and New Zealand. The *Second World* is the Eastern bloc, East Europe and the Soviet Union. Most of the world's hungry people live in the *Third World*, in Central and South America, Africa, most of Asia and the Pacific Islands. Today we sometimes speak of the rich North and the poor South.

What has the Gospel to say about this? Some people may reply, 'Very little.' They believe that the Gospel speaks only about spiritual values. Yet it is a fact that much of the work being done to alleviate poverty in the Third World has been inspired by the Gospel, and is being carried out by active Christians. Many see a direct relationship between the feeding of the hungry world and the community celebration of the Eucharist (Lord's Supper, Communion Service).

His disciples asked him, 'Where in this desert can anyone find enough food to feed all these people?'

Mark 8:4

Christians meet regularly to celebrate the Last Supper of Jesus. They consider this the heart of their worship, their faith and their commitment to their brothers and sisters. They speak of it as a *sacrament*.

> *While they were eating, Jesus took a piece of bread, gave a prayer of thanks, broke it, and gave it to his disciples. 'Take it,' he said, 'this is my body.' Then he took a cup, gave thanks to God, and handed it to them; and they all drank from it. Jesus said, 'This is my blood which is poured out for many, my blood which seals God's covenant...' Then they sang a hymn.*
>
> Mark 14: 22–24, 26

When the Methodist broadcaster, Pauline Webb, visited a village in Chile, a Roman Catholic welcomed her by offering her a piece of bread. In his broken English he said, 'Take, eat.' She saw the invitation as a sort of Eucharist. These are the words used by Christians when they receive bread as the 'Body of Christ'.

A few thoughts

We spend more on hot drinks before we go to bed than we do on foreign aid.

'I'm not interested in the bloody system! Why has he no food? Why is he starving to death?'

Bob Geldof

*The Canadian bishops recently pointed out that a North American steer consumes some 21 pounds of cereal grain to produce one pound of beef; so that Canadians, by eating one hamburger less per week, would make available no less than one million extra tons of grain. This would feed **five million** hungry people.*

'To a people famishing and idle, the only acceptable form in which God can dare appear is work and promise of food and wages.'

M Gandhi

'Half of the people in our world never set foot in school. They have no contact with teachers, and they are deprived of the privilege of becoming dropouts.

Ivan Illich *Deschooling Society* Harper and Row 1971

100 million people have no homes today.
30 million children live on the streets in Third World cities.
50 000 people a day (mainly children), die of slum-related diseases.

Population problems

An argument frequently put forward by the wealthy North is that massive birth control programmes should be introduced in the poor South. Large families only lead to greater poverty. An answer given by those working amongst the starving poor is that the poor need their children. When babies die from simple colds and diarrhoea, parents will want to produce lots of children.

Discuss this complex situation.

Questions and tasks

1   The Communist ideal states *'From every one according to his capacity, to every one according to his need.'* Doesn't that sound like a Christian ideal too?

2   Ask Christian Aid or Cafod to send someone along to talk with your class/group.

3   *'If a person is in extreme necessity, he has the right to take from the riches of others what he himself needs.'* (The Church in the Modern World Vatican II.)

Does this work in practice?

Resources and conservation

Planet earth has limited supplies of air, water, fuel, plants and animal life. Today these vital resources are being used up more quickly than they can be replaced. Modern developments in technology are beginning to cause particular concern because of the massive waste they create. The resulting pollution is exterminating wildlife and even posing a serious threat to human life. Disasters like Chernobyl, of course, are even more threatening.

It is hardly surprising that environmentalists like *Greenpeace*, have become a serious pressure group in politics today. Many Christians support such movements in the conviction that Christianity believes in a God who has given the earth into the care of human beings.

St Francis of Assisi, the man who loved nature, is one of the favourite saints of the Christian Church. He expresses, for the Church, the belief that all creation praises God.

River sealed to save fish

Scientists sealed of River Lark flowing in Cambrid River Ouse in yesterday to stop the st organic pollution wh killed thousands of fi

The operation was fo after a sewage stati — St Edmunds

Nuclear safety

From Mr B. H. Parker,
Sir, Your editorial on "Nuclear ambiguity" (October 2) is critical of the "tide of fear, understandably rising after Chernobyl". Quite so, but we should beware of mindlessly flooding to the defence of nuclear power; that is equally a

Lead pollution falls after additive

The concentratio pollution in the air xhausts has fallen per cent in

Donkey fuel

Dar es Salaam (Reuter) — President Mwinyi told Tanzanian farmers they should use donkeys and ox-carts to transport their crops because the country could not afford the foreign exchange for trucks and petrol.

Fumes knock out

More than 40 people were taken to hospital yest ter a road tanker carrying a corrosive chemical leak. Many collapsed after inhaling fumes from the chemical phenol, an oil-like substance which has a kr out effect similar to that of chloroform.

We plough the fields and scatter
The seeds of suicide
With artificial fertilizer
And insecticide
Our rivers are all poisoned
With jolly effluence
Why can't those men in Whitehall
Have some common sense?
All good gifts around us
Are dying one by one
So thanks you sirs, O thank you sirs
For all that you have done.

(Words by Jeremy Taylor)

'There is sufficiency in the world for man's need but not for man's greed.'

M Gandhi

Questions and tasks

1   Should the world be 'conserved' or 'developed'?
2   Here are some causes of pollution: industrial waste, oil slicks, sewage, littered countryside, lead poisoning, chemical waste into rivers, aerosol cans... Add to this list, and find out all you can about the problem.
3   Contact the *World Wildlife Fund* for information.

Duke warns

Tokyo (Reuter) — The Duke of Edinburgh warned here that the condition of the natural world was getting so bad that "the future of mankind itself is beginning to be at risk".

Health

The progress of medical science has eliminated many health risks from our world. But problems remain.

1   The Third World problem

Millions of people in poor countries suffer from malnutrition. This quickly leads to disease and often to death. Those who don't die from starvation have to face the epidemics following upon poor sanitation, bad water supplies and totally inadequate medical services.

There is some hope. *The World Health Organization*, for example, has achieved sufficient international co-operation to eradicate smallpox. Find out about this organization and the *Food and Agriculture Organization*.

Volunteers from the healthier First and Second Worlds continue to offer medical skills and assistance to the Third World. Amongst these are many Christians, inspired by the healing ministry of Jesus.

> *Jesus healed many who were sick with all kinds of diseases and drove out many demons.*
>
> Mark 1: 34

2   The First World problem

Life in the developed nations has its problems too. For example, the stress and pressure of an industrialized nation produces heart disease. There are medical theories that many conditions are stress-related, even a physical disease like cancer. As fast as progress is made in successfully treating a disease, another type of deadly sickness seems to appear. In this decade it is the AIDS problem.

Good health programmes result in longer life for many. This can create economic problems in our National Health Service.

> Care of the sick has always been a Christian concern. The Roman Catholic Church has a *sacrament* of healing, called the 'Anointing of the sick'.

There have always been some Christians who claim to have the power of healing. How far are doctors and healing ministers working on the same knowledge, but using a different language?

Questions and tasks

1   Find out what you can about care for the elderly. Contact *Help the Aged* and *Age Concern*.

2   Euthanasia or mercy killing (assisted suicide) remains illegal in this country. But some people think it compassionate to put very ill or elderly people 'out of their misery'. What do you think?

3   What is the *Hospice Movement* founded by Cecily Saunders?

Index